SIX RULES OF ULTIMATE WORKFORCE EFFICIENCY

THE FUTURE OF TRUE EMPLOYEE ENGAGEMENT

By Ali Kursun

First published by sparkChief & Co. in 2018

© Copyright 2018 sparkChief & Co.

All rights reserved. No part of this publication may be reproduced, stored in retrieval system or transmitted, in any form or by any means, electronic, photocopying, recording, or otherwise, without the written prior permission of the author.

Note to Librarians: A cataloguing record for this book is available from Swiss National Library (NL) in Switzerland at http://www.helveticat.ch

ISBN 978-1986091138

sparkChief Publishing

This book was published on-demand in cooperation with sparkChief & Co. Publishing. On-demand publishing is a unique process and service of making a book available for retail sale to the public taking advantage of on-demand manufacturing and internet marketing. On-demand publishing includes promotions, retail sales, manufacturing, order fulfilment, accounting and collecting royalties on behalf of the author.

For international book sales:

sparkChief & Co. Publishing

25 Route de Lullier

1254 Jussy, Geneva, SWITZERLAND

phone +41 22 346 24 05; email to bookorders@sparkchief.com

Order online at:

www.sparkchief.com/services_book.html

Also available on amazon.com and other online book sellers.

To the future of people management, which desperately needs radical but common-sense thinking...

TABLE OF CONTENTS

INTRODUCTION Page 3

SECTION 1: KEY CHALLENGES

    Chapter 1: Page 6
    Why CEOs Need to Pay More Attention to the True Cost of Weak Leadership

    Chapter 2: Page 14
    Correlational Leadership and the End of Common Sense

    Chapter 3: Page 18
    Where We Are Spending Corporate Money vs. Where We Should Be

    Chapter 4: Page 27
    The True Cost of Having the Wrong Person in the Job

    Chapter 5: Page 32
    Potential Barriers to Success - and Why We Should Bother

    Chapter 6: Page 39
    Overcoming the Cultural Challenges in Mergers and Acquisitions

Section 2: A New Approach - Six Rules of Ultimate Workforce Efficiency

Chapter 7: Page 46

Rule 1 - Embrace Transparency

- Why More Transparency in Management Practices Is Long Overdue, Inescapable, and Critical for Maximising Shareholder Value

Chapter 8: Page 52

Rule 2 - Empower Leadership Accountability in Everyone

- Why We Need Talented People to Identify Talented People

Chapter 9: Page 55

Rule 3 - Help Your Employees to Learn More About Themselves

- Why Helping Your Employees to Learn More About Themselves Is a Better Solution to Increase and Sustain Engagement in Your Organisation
- What if Every Employee Had a Talent Agent?

Chapter 10: Page 67

Rule 4 - Treat Your Employees Like Your Brand

- Why You Should Treat Employees Like Your Brand, Not Like Your Tangible Assets

Chapter 11: Page 72

Rule 5 - It Is About All Employees, Not Just the Young and Upcoming!

- Leveraging the Generational Potential to Accelerate Growth in All Economies
- Finding and Empowering the Untapped Employee Potential

Chapter 12: Page 86

Rule 6 - Focus on Generating Value for All Stakeholders

- Why Generating Value for All Stakeholders Makes Business Sense

SECTION 3: ACCELERATING CHANGE TO ACHIEVE SUCCESS

Chapter 13: Page 92

The Need for Technology to Accelerate Organisational Alignment

Chapter 14: Page 97

A New Diagnostic to Help Discover the Right Talent

Chapter 15: Page 105
Getting Ready for the Future: The Roadmap

Chapter 16: Page 116
Practical Strategies for Following the Roadmap

Chapter 17: Page 122
Practical Examples of Self-Assessment Users

CONCLUSION AND FUTURE THOUGHTS Page 131

- Keep Your Eyes on the Ball! But Which Ball?

REFERENCES Page 136

INDEX Page 139

ACKNOWLEDGEMENT

My thanks are due to many and various people.

Those who directly supported me with the research and thinking described here and especially Virginia (Ginny) McMorrow, my amazing long-time colleague, friend and editor, who was so instrumental in the way she directed me and helped me to develop this new manuscript.

Many clients, colleagues, and partners contributed to this book over the last couple of years. Finally, my thanks to all who have invited me to speak to them and who remind me that this work really does make a difference.

Many thanks to you all!

INTRODUCTION

Getting your employees "on board" with the company's overall mission and strategic goals is the focus of this book, leading toward optimisation of resources, budgets, and employee talent. Common sense decrees that without employees who are engaged and motivated – and aligned – with the company's desires and needs, the organisation will not perform to its potential, revenues will falter, and market shares decline.

The challenge that such an alignment entails is ever-present and complex, though the difficulties it represents are not insurmountable. As illustrated in the first section of the book, there is a critical need for CEOs to understand the link between weak leadership and its true cost to all stakeholders – the management team, employee base, and shareholders. Part of the problem involves where corporations spend money – often, unfortunately, on human resources programmes that do little or nothing to further the development of the individual employee. Without such forward movement, innovativeness and creativity stagnate, causing a drag on the quality and reliability of the company's products and services. Another source of unwise spending is recruiting, hiring, and training employees who do not "fit" the culture or do not have the requisite talent. Finally, this section will explore the cultural dilemmas presented by mergers and acquisitions, a clear situation where cultures and missions are likely to clash.

In recognition of these challenges, the second section of the book discusses a new approach: six rules of ultimate workforce efficiency. The rules are these:

- Embrace transparency in management practices.
- Empower leadership accountability in all employees, not just the management team.
- Help employees learn more about their needs and desires and how the company and employees can benefit from this awareness.
- Treat employees like the company brand.
- Leverage all employee segments, age groups, and untapped potential.
- Focus on generating value for all stakeholders.

Technology and its viable solutions to optimising the alignment between leadership goals and employee needs represent the final section of the book. The need for technology in today's swift-moving world is obvious, offering an effective approach to helping management find, hire, and engage the most suitable talent. A discussion of the sparkChief™ methodology, along with practical strategies for its implementation and case studies that illustrate its usefulness, completes the section.

In conclusion, defining the problem, understanding the possible solutions, and taking proactive steps are all markers on the roadmap to a win-win scenario for your company. Join us on that road….

SECTION 1:
KEY CHALLENGES

CHAPTER 1
WHY CEOS NEED TO PAY MORE ATTENTION TO THE TRUE COST OF WEAK LEADERSHIP

The definition of leadership in modern origination has evolved over the last 20 years, becoming very exclusive rather than inclusive. Merriam-Webster's traditional meaning is "a position as a leader of a group, organisation, etc. ... the power or ability to lead other people." In line with that definition, 91% of respondents to the Millennial Leadership Study[1] aspire to be a leader. While almost half of the millennials queried define leadership as "empowering others to succeed," 43% said their biggest motivator to be a leader was to empower others.

These noble sentiments, however, miss a critical point. Every person is, or should be, his or her own leader. Believing that only a few qualified people have the right to be a leader is inherently incorrect. To be a responsible family member, community member, citizen, employee, colleague, business manager, or executive, every individual must be a personal leader. If they are not, how can people claim to lead others? Understanding that one should not seek leadership in others is the starting point to truly strive toward having a better family, community, society, organisation, corporation, and nation.

---
[1] Conducted by WorkplaceTrends.com and Virtuali.

Should the status quo change with a new definition of leadership, consider the tremendous responsibility it would place on the shoulders of parents, community leaders, government officials, corporate shareholders, and executives. Nevertheless, this key transformation should be a top priority. If ignored, weak leadership in any endeavour has the potential to rapidly consume our natural, human, and financial resources.

This reinvented definition is urgent, vital, and the most important ingredient to achieving fulfillment and success in our personal lives, communities, societies, and organisations. Every passing day is lost to mediocracy, unhappiness, inefficiency, conflict, untapped human effort, and underperforming organisations. Without individuals accepting the challenge to take the lead on a personal level, no sustainable solution exists to our diverse problems.

The Problem with the Status Quo

Companies around the globe are experiencing a growing talent gap at the executive level. According to the Global Workforce Leadership Survey[2], 46% of respondents said that leadership was the skill that was the most difficult to find in their workforce. In fact, only one-third (36%) listed leadership as an existing skill in their organisations.

An analysis of responses by U.S. businesses and HR leaders to a 2016 global study[3] showed a critical need to improve leadership

---

[2] Conducted by Saba and WorkplaceTrends.com.

development initiatives. Although U.S. respondents made up nearly one-third of the 7,500 global respondents, their answers generally mirrored responses from other world regions. "The best thought-out business strategy will fail miserably if the leaders within an organisation don't have the skills to make it come to fruition," said Dennis Baltzley, senior client partner and global head of leadership development solutions for Korn Ferry Hay Group. The study found that only:

- 17% were confident they have the right leadership capabilities in place to execute on strategy.

- 18% were confident that their leadership team demonstrated the behaviours needed to successfully deliver on strategic business priorities.

Such studies point to the problem with today's status quo. Unfortunately, the majority of people have defaulted to average performance in many aspects of their lives. At the very best, people appear to be content with mediocre activity and results in every plan they put forward. We convince each other that if our peers are similar to us, then that should be the norm. How could we even think of doing better?

Our understanding of outperformance has shaped into some sort of magic. We seek only science in the tangible world and call the intangible world an art form that is difficult to measure. We shy

---

[3] Conducted by the Hay Group division of Korn Ferry.

away from the unknown without bothering to explore what is possible. Because of this lack of personal leadership – combined with our acceptance of average outcomes – the problems and difficulties we face continue to accumulate. This approach, or thinking by default, breeds mediocracy.

Over the last 20 years, this backward thinking has prevailed as we become content with our future, encouraging the emergence of disengaged family members, community members, citizens, employees, and executives. The conclusion? Nobody cares. This dangerous thinking carries an enormous price tag, a cost hidden from corporate or government income statements and balance sheets.

The Root Cause of the Problem

In a nutshell, the root cause of the status quo comes down to these factors: our misconceived incentive philosophy combined with weak leadership bred by this misalignment in our families, communities, organisations, and governments.

The most critical question every CEO needs to ask, regardless of organisational type or size, is how do we want our incentive philosophy to work? Incentive philosophy is not about how a company rewards its people. Rather, it is about knowing how your people should work to achieve a shared outcome. If managers do not deeply understand why and how their people work within an organised structure, then managers can do anything they want, yet still not achieve optimal performance.

> ### The Real Meaning of Performance Plus
>
> Optimal performance is about maximum return, whether financial, personal, or societal. Maximum return is not about what peers or the market holds that one can achieve – for example, 3% to 5% annual growth (although with today's norms, these numbers are considered great) or beating peers or the market by another 3% or 5% – which is a mediocre thought. Maximum return is about significant outperformance, about multiples, never a small percentage differential.

Engaging the Disengaged

To achieve optimal results, it is clear that employees who are motivated and engaged have a strong connection to an organisation's productivity, profitability, and viability as a player in the market. According to a recent Gallup survey, only 32% of employees are engaged at work, with 50.8% not engaged. In fact, engagement statistics have been flat for the past 15 years. These appalling statistics indicate a misalignment throughout the corporate world brought about by misalignment of incentives. What use are incentives if they do not work? Companies that outperform significantly better align their incentive philosophy than those that perform or underperform – an amazingly efficient approach to outperformance.

There appears to be more to outperformance than simply offering rewards to deserving individuals, although rewards remain a very important tool to support motivation to achieve results. That said, however, it is long past time for managers to resist using their favorite medicine to solve difficult problems: the "reward pill."

Companies dole out this particular medication as pharmacists distribute Aspirin for various ills, including headache, stomach ache, and blood thinning. In organisational terms, the reward pill seeks to resolve promotion, retention, and hiring issues. But remember, in neither health care nor employee care, the pill is not a cure; it only eliminates the symptoms. In fact, one should not even need to take a pill if the root cause of the problem is effectively addressed.

The Gap Between Personal and Organisational Goals

The truth behind underperformance and misalignment of incentives/rewards lies in the misalignment of personal and organisational goals. If one is not clear about personal goals in life, it becomes difficult to discuss shared goals between an individual and the organisation to which the person belongs.

Thus, we needlessly consume resources (personal or corporate) when individuals work for the wrong organisation or managers hire the wrong person to achieve a set of specific objectives for the organisation. Mountains of submissions from unqualified candidates overwhelm business managers and HR staff, waste time and money, and often lead to bad decisions. The search for hidden talent, particularly in leadership positions, can uncover the leaders – the individuals who lead themselves, as well as possess the capability to lead others – through the use of technology that can match individuals' skills and desires and vision with what a company really wants and needs to go boldly into the future.

What has become the norm of mediocre outcomes and outlooks no longer serves all stakeholders (shareholders, employees, employers, governments, and other partners we work with to generate value). While it benefits an exclusive few individuals who have become professional experts who think of value creation only as a personal endeavour to lead others, CEOs should not allow this breed to prosper at the cost of all other stakeholders. Shareholders and boards should make CEOs accountable for hiring only the leaders who share this new vision of the future organisation. It is only then that we will have a chance to change and improve – by finding and cultivating talent who can take charge of their own growth while empowering others to achieve shared goals.

The Storm and Its Aftermath

Complacency prevails. To change the interpretation of leadership to effectively nurture the right individuals requires open-mindedness and courage. Rarely do people happily accept change, and this new thinking will be transformational, arriving like an unwelcome storm. But after the winds die down and the sun reappears, we will rebuild as we always do, relying on the human need to move forward.

The result will be worthwhile. Organisations will survive longer and succeed far better than those of prior years, which have often faded into oblivion. And individuals will be more successful in their ability to lead fulfilling personal and career lives, while encouraging others to join in a united effort to better themselves and the organisations with which they interact.

CHAPTER 2

CORRELATIONAL LEADERSHIP AND THE END OF COMMON SENSE

Leadership is such an overused term that it has become an exclusive synonym for seniority or senior management, now struggling for meaning and respect in the corporate world. Today's organisations are so well-designed that they almost run on autopilot, with existing management systems and policies leaving almost no room for error. At the very least, these institutions are stable and immune to short-term deterioration without any remarkable effort because we have all come to value and appreciate regular and consistent results. In addition, compliance supervision and regulation make it difficult in typical situations for a modern organisation to mess it all up.

However, this scenario does not necessarily imply that the organisation is performing at the optimum level with efficient use of resources, both financial and human. In fact, regular and consistent results may simply point to just-acceptable performance. In any case, leadership continues to reap financial rewards, which may or may not be truly earned; after all, it has become very difficult to measure the true impact of any given leadership role. In the majority of cases, people believe that things happen because of their authoritative influence and decisions, not necessarily because of the other people around them. In light of this situation, it seems apparent that what is needed is an investigation into the true impact of a leader in isolation.

Checking the Facts

Decisions taken by leaders obviously have a significant impact on organisation results, for better or worse, but, can organisations directly link the results to such actions? So many companies go bust or perform at their lowest level because of bad decisions made by weak leaders – resulting in bad performance, unhappiness, dissatisfaction, wastefulness, inefficiency, untapped potential, poor customer service, no innovation, little motivation, and so on. One wonders if the average results of the many leaders do not actually link to specific cause and effect, but rather to correlations. In other words, the business community has created and accepted a new leadership definition that is purely based on correlation.

Logic and conventional wisdom are as follows: Company results are "acceptable," so I (the business leader) should belong to the "good leader club." But, in reality, no one has a clue whether those results were, in fact, caused by the leader or by the very well-established management systems already in place. If the result is due to the management systems and policies, then we are paying that leader a super-premium in terms of bonuses and other perquisites for something that was not worthwhile.

Unfortunately, many organisations do not measure this significant unknown factor, which automatically correlates company performance with leadership without validating the actual cause and effect. That said, a company could simply place any person with some intelligence into a leadership role for the same results. In other words, this conventional wisdom has led to correlation leadership – not causal – in many organisations.

The Road to Nowhere - or Success?

By not demanding the analysis of cause and effect in our organisations, we are traveling on a road that leads to the end of common sense and optimal performance. Consider:

- Shouldn't boards of trustees or directors hold leaders accountable for specific, measurable goals?
- If the results of a company cannot be linked to the actual decisions and strategies of a particular leader or team of leaders, where does the blame or praise truly belong?
- How can boards grant generous compensation and benefits to leaders that may or may not exert any influence on average results?

Correlational leadership can, sadly, only lead to encouragement of average performance and lack of motivation. When such thinking starts at the top, it soon trickles down through all levels of employees, who do not feel empowered to become their own leaders. Why should they bother, if adequate/average performance still nets rewards for their managers?

In the end, leadership – whether individual or organisational – demands responsibility, accountability, and the urge to do more, be more, and perform more. Personal accountability – cause and effect – is the driver that can return common sense to leadership.

CHAPTER 3

WHERE WE ARE SPENDING CORPORATE MONEY VS. WHERE WE SHOULD BE

No matter how financially successful a company may be, smart leaders know how to spend funds wisely, efficiently, and effectively. Yet, so many organisations squander their budgets with little or no reward when it comes to hiring and retaining the best talent.

Companies worldwide continue to struggle with the problem of employee engagement. An article in the Harvard Business Review[4] cites a survey that analysed responses from 200,000 employees across 40 companies in 60 countries. The research found unsettling results: Employees with the deepest knowledge of the company typically are the least engaged, and highly engaged senior executives are likely to underestimate the discontent on the front lines.

With that unhappy finding, one wonders what employers are spending money on – at least those organisations that strive to address employee disengagement? Budgets traditionally go toward

---

[4] Rob Markey, "The Four Secrets to Employee Engagement," Harvard Business Review (January 27, 2014), citing a survey by Bain & Company, in conjunction with Netsurvey.

training, benefits, rewards, and other typical components of an employee package.

For example, U.S. training expenditures—including payroll and spending on external products and services—took an upward trajectory, soaring 14.2% to US$70.6 billion.[5] Beneficiaries of various training programmes included executives (10%), managers/exempt (22%), non-managers/exempt (32%), and non-exempt employees (39%). The cost for training can be high, according to "HR Factbook 2015: Benchmarks and Trends for U.S. Organisations": Mature human resources organisations – integrated into the business – spend US$4,434 per employee on average, compared with just US$2,112 among those at the lowest level of maturity.[6]

In addition, global employers spend, on average, 31% of employee salary. Unfortunately, in spite of this hefty outlay, well-meaning benefits are often misdirected, as illustrated by the following statistics[7]:

- While nearly 90% of employers view attracting talent and improving engagement as their top objectives when offering employee benefits, only 7% of global human

---

[5] 2015 Training Industry Report, cited in Training Magazine (November-December 2015).
[6] Press release, "US HR Organisations Spending Increases, Following a Rise in Employee Turnover" (January 14, 2015).
[7] Stephen Miller, "Missing the Mark: Employees Don't Appreciate Benefits Spending," SHRM.org (October 3, 2016), citing Thomson's Online Benefits report, Global Employee Benefits Watch 2016/17.

resources professionals consistently deliver against their benefits plan objectives.

- Nearly half (46%) do not use analytics when devising and managing their benefits strategies.
- Human resources teams struggle to make communications relevant to a globally diverse employee base, but often fail to make their messaging personal enough to resonate with their target audience. The proof? Over 60% of employees are dissatisfied with their benefit plans.
- Almost 70% of employees in global organisations want benefits around key life stages, but only 46% of employers use this opportunity to engage with their workforce.

Overall, companies spend over US$720 million each year on employee engagement, a figure that is projected to rise to over US$1.5 billion. Once again, despite the huge outflow of funds, employee engagement is at record lows — 13% according to Gallup[8].

The Need for a Different Accounting System

To get a better handle on the success of company strategies, an article in the McKinsley Quarterly suggested a forward-looking alterative.[9] "Companies focus far too much on measuring returns on invested capital (ROIC) rather than on measuring the contributions

---

[8] Susan LaMotte, "Employee Engagement Depends on What Happens Outside of the Office," Harvard Business Review (January 13, 2015).
[9] Lowell Bryan, "The New Metrics of Corporate Performance Profit per Employee," McKinsley Quarterly (February 2007).

made by their talented people. The vast majority of companies still gauge their performance using systems ... based on metrics that don't take sufficient notice of the real engines of wealth creation today: the knowledge, relationships, reputations, and other intangibles created by talented people and represented by investments in such activities as R&D, marketing, and training."

An analysis of industry averages, in the following chart, provides an interesting perspective on revenue per employee.[10] Oil and gas companies make at least twice as much revenue per employee than other sectors, while healthcare and utilities companies also have high ratios. A possible explanation involves the cost of doing business. Oil and gas companies spend billions of dollars on capital expenditures to build and maintain plants and rigs, while paying extra taxes and royalties. Healthcare companies spend a lot on R&D to stay competitive, while utilities maintain vast amounts of infrastructure. These sectors generally hire specialised employees and pay higher salaries for such expertise and knowledge.

---

[10] Jeff Desjardins, visualcapitalist.com (June 15, 2017).

Rank	Sector	Avg. Revenue Per Employee (US$)
#1	Energy	$1.79 million
#2	Healthcare	$0.89 million
#3	Utilities	$0.81 million
#4	Consumer Staples	$0.70 million
#5	Financials	$0.65 million
#6	Telecommunications	$0.61 million
#7	Materials	$0.60 million
#8	Tech	$0.48 million
#9	Consumer Discretionary	$0.42 million
#10	Industrials	$0.32 million

What, Then, Should Companies Spend Their Money On?

The answer lies not so much on implementing costly programmes or purchasing expensive tools, but in taking practical, common sense steps.

Author Susan LaMotte[11] opines: "Perhaps human resources leaders are spending their money in the wrong places. When we only try to understand and affect what happens at work, we ignore the most basic tenet of person-organisation fit: employees bring their whole selves to work. What happens after the workday may be just as important as during it." She offers inexpensive suggestions for employers:

- Find new insights using existing data. For example, if early morning or late afternoon standing meetings are driving significant disengagement, perhaps the majority of employees have long commutes. Or, if your employees are hesitant to take vacation, it may be that they are saving it for personal issues like childcare struggles.
- Ask different questions. If your surveys and other interventions focus on work, expand the question set to understand employees' lives outside work – internal values,

---

[11] Susan LaMotte, "Employee Engagement Depends on What Happens Outside of the Office," Harvard Business Review (January 13, 2015).
[12] Steve Crabtree, "Untapped Human Capital Is the Next Great Global Resource," Gallup.com blog (January 22, 2018).

family needs, commuting time and methods, and personal interests.

From a global perspective,[12] confirming the need for a change in direction, a Gallup.com author explained: "The need to make better use of the human capital in organisations – from small businesses to entire societies -- has never been more evident than in the years since the Great Recession. ... Leaders worldwide faced the realisation that to cushion against the severe shocks that can come with global boom-and-bust cycles, they need to diversify their economies and better use the untapped potential within their populations. ... As more of the world moves toward knowledge-based economies in which companies automate many routinised jobs, competitive advantage increasingly depends on the effectiveness with which businesses develop and deploy their human capital – that is, their employees' knowledge, skills, and talents." The author confirmed the disheartening trend that most organisations are unsuccessful in meeting this need – that is, Gallup's State of the Global Workplace report found that just 15% of employees worldwide are engaged in their jobs.

Further, "Because many organisations are automating roles, a higher proportion of the remaining jobs involve specialised knowledge and skills. That means," the author continued, "employees have greater potential to increase their value by

acquiring education and experiences that make them more effective in their particular niche in their organisation. Great managers recognise this and understand that it requires them to establish more personalised relationships with their team members than traditional management theory may call for." The author cites two "relics" of outdated management that no longer work:

- Annual performance reviews. Contrast these infrequent, structured conversations with development-focused cultures that regard managers as coaches, offering more frequent dialogue with individual employees.

- Promoting employees to manage others, based on seniority. This practice often does not consider the new manager's talent (or lack of it) to act as effective leaders.

Putting Money to Optimal Use

Whether or not corporate funds are abundant, leadership should recognise the urgency to allocate this resource in ways that will garner the most profitable results in terms of revenue, shareholder satisfaction, and employee engagement. Throwing money at traditional human resources systems and approaches that have been proven to fail (or, succeed only minimally) is not the answer to ensuring alignment of employees with corporate strategies.

A key ingredient of success is getting to know your workforce. If you understand the needs and desires of your employees, in conjunction with company goals, the result will prove beneficial to all parties. Listening, interacting, and responding – essentially, communicating – represent the commonsense approach to determining how best to engage lacklustre employees.

CHAPTER 4

THE TRUE COST OF HAVING THE WRONG PERSON IN THE JOB

Internal and external hiring mistakes happen more often than one likes to believe. Unfortunately, a significant percentage of hiring decisions are the result of the hiring manager's "gut" feelings or intense pressure to fill a vacancy swiftly. When qualified candidates are few and far between, managers must make a selection from a pool of individuals who do not necessarily possess behavioural or hard skills such as knowledge or hands-on experience. And, at times, HR, the line manager, or both, may find themselves fooled by a candidate's appearance, blatant close relationship to management, and interviewing skills, or pressed to consider a colleague's referral, without digging deeper to ascertain the underlying fitness for the position.

Many leaders fail to understand the true cost of hiring and retaining individuals who either do not have the necessary credentials, behavioural aptitude, and experience or, perhaps, are unwilling to exchange acceptable work for the salary they earn. Such costs, often overlooked, can only lead to the long-term detriment of the organisation, risking its viability and success going forward.

The Short-term Estimate

An article[13] on employment costs refers to an expensive hiring mistake – the cost of a "mis-hire" – as the unconscious avoidance, denial, and/or toleration of underperforming or destructive employees. The higher the position level, the quicker the cost of a such an error increases exponentially. Brad Smart, Founder, Topgrading, Inc., cited in the article, considers the potential cost for a mis-hire as:

- 14 times salary for employees earning a base salary under US$100,000

- 28 times salary for employees earning US$100,000 to US$250,000

Besides the typical direct and indirect costs of dealing with the challenge of finding new, qualified employees (such as recruiting, interviewing, reference checking, lost productivity in beginning months, and so on), employers need to consider long-term opportunity costs – for example, substandard service; lowered employee morale and substandard performance in other employees due to passive resistance; missed deadlines; customer dissatisfaction with product quality, customer service, lack of innovation caused

---

[13] Denise Corcoran, "Shocking Costs of Hiring Mistakes," Empowered Business.com (October 30, 2013).

by disengagement and/or lost trust/faith in the company; and, unfortunately, missed sales opportunities.

The Long-Term Financial Implications

Imagine a business unit that has an annual revenue of US$250 million, operating at a 15% margin. Led by 12 global/regional leaders who cost, on average, US$300,000 per head, the impact of mis-hiring a single leader for the team can be truly devastating for the business unit. Two mis-hires will be a big problem. Three will result in long-term damage.

Using this data as the base for an example calculation, the business impact becomes even more clear.

Scenario	# of Mis-hires	Total Cost (US$) of Mis-hires *Cost of 1 Mis-hire at $300,000 (average salary) x 28*
1	Cost of 1 Mis-hire	8.4 million
2	Cost of 2 Mis-hires	16.8 million
3	Cost of 3 Mis-hires	25.2 million

Consequently, the potential financial impact of mis-hires on a business unit with an annual revenue of US$250 million at a 15%

operating margin (or, 250,000,000 x 15% = 37,500,000) can be as significant as a 67% reduction of the operating margin.

The hypothetical impact on the company's operating margin is as follows, using the same three scenarios.

Scenario	Assumption: Total cost of Mis-hires ÷ operating margin	Reduction on Operating Margin
1	8.4 million ÷ 37.5 million	22.4%
2	16.8 million ÷ 37.5 million	44.8%
3	25.2 million ÷ 37.5 million	67.2%

This result represents a huge impact on the organisation's bottom line, considering the efforts and assets invested in such a business. Not only the leadership team, but shareholders as well, should be very concerned with scenarios that adversely affect profits and growth. The last thing shareholders desire is to risk the percentage of their return on their investment, which would be unacceptable. More to the point, the last thing executives desire is to find themselves, in turn, hunting for new jobs as a result of their incompetent and inefficient management of the entity.

Cost Transparency Is Key

Put this way, in light of actual numbers, the financial impact of mis-hires is a very clear, troubling, and compelling story. A serious issue faced by many organisations today involves the lack of transparency with regard to actual costs or, indeed, little or no attempt to search for the true impact.

Non-transparency triggers extensive hidden costs that take the form of wasted resources, financial expenditures, and lost time for all stakeholders – from the employee to the leadership team to shareholders. Hidden or not, these costs take a toll on all of us as we continue, over and over, to pay them.

CHAPTER 5

POTENTIAL BARRIERS TO SUCCESS – AND WHY WE SHOULD BOTHER

It would be naïve not to consider the barriers to success when implementing any new approach to develop leadership, accountability, and self-awareness in order to boost the success of – and align – our personal and organisational efforts. Therefore, it makes sense to identify these potential barriers as potential hurdles and then develop strategies to mitigate the risks involved. These new approaches not only involve making things right, but also confirm that there is indeed a better way to succeed and that we want the best for every stakeholder without exception. Among the potential barriers are the following factors.

Barrier 1: Shareholder Philosophy

I do not know of any explicit shareholder philosophy based on mediocre performance expectations. After all, the main reason people invest in a business is to obtain maximum returns on their invested capital. Further, I am not aware of any explicit shareholder approach that wishes ill on other stakeholders and focuses instead solely on personal financial outcomes.

Investors (people) like to talk about their investments and the choices they make in terms of growing their capital. In the majority of cases, especially in publicly-traded and family-controlled investments, investors, without exception, seek new ways to increase profits and improve margins. They keep a close eye on how management executes their investment strategy.

However, shareholders are not always well-informed, particularly when it comes to large organisations. Although the purpose of the board and management team is to safeguard the interests of investors, by law (in a majority of jurisdictions), shareholders also expect them to respect certain operational ethics. On the surface, there should not be any suspension of intentional resistance to new approaches from the shareholders' perspective – that is, shareholders cannot explicitly intend to exploit the workforce for their own gains without honouring the right of each employee to achieve self-knowledge and fulfil the individual's potential.

Yet, on the other hand, explicit intentions sometimes may not be authentic; although legally justified, they implicitly drive the purpose of a given investment to satisfy only shareholders' gains. Whether or not this type of implicit intention is agreed or even articulated behind closed doors is another matter for investigation beyond the scope of this discussion. However, if suspension is perceived, there is very little potential for the executive team to attempt new approaches that would jeopardise shareholders' current investment philosophy.

Barrier 2: Current Leadership and Management Intentions

If current shareholders have explicit and implicit intentions to consider all other stakeholders' interests along with their own to maximise returns for all stakeholders, management's key focus need only be guarding the interest of all stakeholders. Management's role in delivering returns while safeguarding the interest of all stakeholders should link to management's ability to be as transparent as possible. With management under constant scrutiny by the board, having a specific mandate from shareholders to manage the operations of their investment with optimum efficiency, it is common sense for the organisation's leadership to continuously seek productivity gains. By explicit default, the expectation for the management team is that they serve all stakeholders (shareholders, management, employees, clients, suppliers, and so on) and fulfil their accountability by facilitating a value generation for all.

The only problem with such facilitation is that, as an orchestrator, while aiming to safeguard the interest of all stakeholders, management might attempt to benefit more than other stakeholders. I do not know of any explicit intentional desire by any management team to achieve personal gains (although there have been disappointments in certain organisations, I prefer to assume that these are exceptions). However, if there is any implicit desire for personal gains, such people, in my opinion, belong in prison rather than on management teams. Legal means should address implicitly-driven leadership or management teams who only guard their own interests. In essence, management should support innovative approaches to maximise returns for all stakeholders.

Barrier 3: Existing Employee Population Disposition

The key purpose of any employee in working for any type of organisation is to generate value for all stakeholders. Although the definition of value may differ by entity, the key purpose remains the same. No employee should explicitly seek only personal gain. Fortunately, legal implications and internal management policies exist to address such acts. However, as some employees may have implicit intentions, at the very least, an organisation that recognises such patterns of behaviour should discharge such employees.

Although many reasons can explain why some employees focus on generating value only for their own gains, the typical rationalisation is that they are encouraged to do so or live in a working environment that implicitly allows such behaviour. Obviously, other personally driven reasons may exist due to individual inclinations. However, the fact remains that such employees will resist transparency and will misguide others around them, causing frustration throughout the organisation. Management needs to identify such individuals as early as possible to avoid their preventing the company from deploying new approaches.

Barrier 4: Political Environment in Which One Lives

If one's country has an unstable political environment or discourages freedom of expression, it becomes challenging to advocate self-discovery and awareness. Some governments thrive solely on that promise, not wanting citizens to be more self-aware or to excel due to their knowledge of personal capabilities. Organisations established in these markets face the same problems.

Barrier 5: Current Educational Systems

Unfortunately, many current education systems are archaic and based on an outdated economic model. There has been no large-scale transformational change in either developed or emerging markets regarding education. Learning still involves delivery of specific content and methods that are, unfortunately, not suited to every individual. Education does not provide adequate options for many students and lacks personalisation, representing a considerable barrier to preparing the younger generation for the future and facilitating their personal progress.

There is an urgency to alter and improve education systems in almost every country. If there is no action to modify these systems to address the needs of today's generation, schools will continue to produce unhappy and frustrated individuals in society. Self-discovery and awareness should be at the core of future system transformations.

Reasons to Push Through the Barriers – For Individuals

In light of the struggle and hurdles to make changes to move forward, it may seem easier to accept the status quo and settle for a life and career of mediocrity. But isn't that a waste of one's potential for happiness and success?

Self-actualisation, self-fulfillment, self-awareness, happiness – whatever one considers to be an optimal state – has benefits that impact all aspects not only of one's own life, but also those with whom we interact, be it our family, co-workers, friends, and the community at large.

Self-awareness and personal empowerment should be an individual's priority, as they form the foundation from which we can move forward on the path to making life-affirming decisions.

Reasons to Push Through the Barriers – For Employers

Employers – and other organisational entities – have a strong motivation to ensure that their employees have the opportunities to advance along their personal development path. In the end, employee growth can only serve to support the company's strategic goals – as long as they are compatible. In a recent article of the Gallup Business Journal,[14] Gallup's research showed that companies with engaged workforces have higher earnings per share (EPS) and recovered from the 2008 recession at a faster rate.

---

[14] Susan Sorenson, "Employee Engagement Drives Growth" (June 20, 2013).

Businesses with a critical mass of engaged employees outperformed their competition.

Barriers Are Not Insurmountable

Acknowledging the genuine hurdles faced on both an individual and organisational level, the human condition strives upward and forward. Cooperation among people and organisations – whether community or job or government-related – can address the issues, given time, resources, and the right tools. In this day and age, technology is one of those tools that can support the path to empowerment, leadership, and self-awareness.

CHAPTER 6

OVERCOMING THE CULTURAL CHALLENGES IN MERGERS AND ACQUISITIONS

Numerous studies indicate that many merger and acquisition (M&A) deals fail to meet financial expectations – a figure that can vary from 50% to as high as 90%. According to McKinsey research,[15] 70% of mergers do not achieve their expected "revenue synergies."

Know What Your Employees Think Before Shaking Hands

Why do M&As fail? One author suggests a number of pitfalls[16] that can thwart success, one of which involves assigning the chief financial officer or general counsel to act as the "M&A champion." Such individuals, already overwhelmed by the responsibilities of their demanding positions, may not have the time to do a proper job of due diligence. Other underlying reasons for failure or lacklustre performance[17] include overpaying for the deal, lacking strategic clarity, making slow decisions, implementing poor

---

[15] Cited by Neil Hodge, "Why Do M&As Fail?", Risk Management Magazine (April 3, 2017).
[16] Marvin Dumon, "8 Reasons M&A Deals Fall Through," Investopedia.com.
[17] "How 'Good' Deals Go Bad: The Most Common Causes of M&A Failures," Mergerintegration.com.

integration planning and execution, eroding business fundamentals, allowing competitors to steal customers and market share, and losing key talent. And yet, in spite of that last factor being a reason for failure, talent acquisition – as the rationale for a deal – has more than doubled in importance, rising from 4% to 9%, since the spring of 2016.[18]

Leadership often views talent – one of the key ingredients in any successful enterprise – as a "soft issue" when it comes to business deals. And yet, cultural integration of merging organisations – their missions, values, goals, and workforce – remains as one of the top challenges. Despite the goodwill of both parties, many deal makers misread their own and the new company's culture, unaware of the true nature of their employees. With this lack of knowledge, they falsely believe that the two cultures will fit together seamlessly after a brief interval of time.

Traditionally, to gain knowledge and accurate facts, the M&A team performs extensive due diligence on a potential technology, service, or product to evaluate essential factors (such as financial records), along with anything else deemed material. Yet, unfortunately, insufficient rigor goes into assessing cultural alignment despite the fact that culture assessment and alignment, leadership assessment, talent retention, benefits, and compensation are part and parcel of the due diligence process. Such factors often undergo a superficial evaluation.

---

[18] "The State of the Deal: M&A Trends 2018," Deloitte.

Adding to the problem, it is not uncommon for decision makers to depend on both companies' senior management perspectives and assumptions when it comes to cultural issues, often falling short of any objective factual observation on the matter. Or, at the very best, they try to gain organisational insights into each other by tackling observable, tangible matters, such as[19]:

- Organisation development: functional and reporting relationship charts
- Employee relations: potential disputes; employment agreements with officers, directors, key employees, criminal proceedings or significant civil litigation involvement of key employees and officers, and appropriateness of the company's treatment of personnel
- Compensation: pay schedules to officers, directors, and key employees; management incentive or bonus plans; deferred compensation
- Benefits: health, medical, life, retirement, severance or termination pay, vacation, and sick leave
- Administration: employment manuals and policies
- Merger-related items: retention arrangements with key employees, and layoffs and resultant severance costs

---

[19] Richard D. Harroch and David A. Lipkin, "20 Key Due Diligence Activities in a Merger and Acquisition Transaction," Forbes.com (December 19, 2014).

As such, however, they totally disregard the need to gain true insights through a deeper understanding of company culture – a deeper comprehension of what makes their organisation function.

"Hard" Approaches Can Make the Difference

The bottom line is that information – about employee desires, goals, commitment, and alignment to the company – is critical and, sadly, often lacking. New approaches and tools are a positive way to support informed decision making and shed more light into gaining a more accurate assessment of company culture.

Part of the dilemma in considering new methods is that due diligence on people issues typically focuses on top and senior management perspectives, especially in determining how senior managers in both organisations will work together or take new roles in the new entity. Little to limited worthy effort is spent on layers below senior management. The downside in taking this approach is the assumption that leadership has a clear view of the entire organisation, from managers on down to non-exempt employees. In the end, deal makers base their decisions on mere assumptions of a very limited number of people in both parties rather than on the full big picture.

To broaden those assumptions and get to know the workforce, new approaches and tools can help objectively assess cultural fit or alignment, rather than having deal makers depend on anecdotal or self-biased perspectives. With costly efforts made to uncover the facts about a product, service, or technology, how can managers not do the same for their workforce? When one thinks about the high stakes involved in any M&A deal, financial and human, it is imperative to expend a greater effort to assess the whole organisation. Without a viable and objective assessment of facts at hand when making people decisions, leadership faces an enormous risk for failure, accompanied by wasted time, resources, finances, and human talent.

And the waste can be significant. With no coordinated retention actions taken, for example, one study found that 47% of all senior managers in an acquired firm leave within the first year.[20] Beyond that, within the first three years, 72% are on their way out as well. Added to this cost are other factors: employees who remain but underperform, having lost commitment to their job or organisation. To retain valuable talent and minimise such appalling losses, deal makers should recognise that employees need to feel secure and important, be able to provide input, have control over options, understand the "why" of the merger and their place in the new structure.

It does not make sense to discuss whether two company cultures are compatible before even knowing what these two cultures represent. In addition, as company culture is such a broad term, it makes absolutely no sense to refer to it as a singular carved-in-stone definition. There are almost as many cultures as there are

---

[20] "How to Retain Key Talent in an Acquisition," Mergerintegration.com.

employees in any organisation. Therefore, there is no point of talking about culture compatibility if one does not truly understand one's existing culture and workforce.

Extra Effort Minimises the Risk of Failure

The problem may simply be that cultural challenges are considered "soft" issues that do not have "hard" answers. After all, soft issues fall into the intangible realm, poised to be shaped in any way people want them to be. And that is the moment that logic is lost and deal makers deviate from an effective decision-making process.

However, it does not have to be this way. Technology and common sense together can help leadership overcome many cultural issues through the use of better, more accurate assessment tools. Gaining a deeper understanding of people's true aspirations and aligning that with the new company's strategic priorities is a much more powerful approach than just basing decisions on a handful of people who have an approximate and self-biased approach to cultural assessment.

SECTION 2:
A NEW APPROACH - SIX RULES OF ULTIMATE WORKFORCE EFFICIENCY

CHAPTER 7

RULE 1 - EMBRACE TRANSPARENCY

Why More Transparency in Management Practices Is Long Overdue, Inescapable, and Critical for Maximising Shareholder Value

This era may be the most exciting time for management practices – but only if leadership can truly commit to taking appropriate action. As technology transforms the way we live and work, we are closer and closer to reaching that goal we have been preaching about and striving toward for a long time. That goal is simply to bring more transparency in management practices in order to maximise returns for all key stakeholders – all – not only leadership and investment shareholders.

Technological advancement, not voluntary leadership, has indirectly driven this movement toward transparency. In addition, every field has witnessed three factors that have added to the momentum: the need to boost productivity, increase efficiency, and improve return on capital invested. As technology has pushed the boundaries of maximising business profitability, it has also transformed the rules of collaboration, competitive advantage through the democratisation of creativity, and the dynamics of sharing outcomes. Nevertheless, transparency is not yet fully here.

Resistance Is Unproductive

In spite of the driving forces, the need to become transparent in certain areas of management was inevitable, anyway. This movement represents the most significant evolution of all time for management practices. Although technology in time will continue to bring more openness and transparency in our lives, communities, societies, corporations, and nations, the unfortunate truth is that the result may not be something that everyone desires. Nevertheless, we need to empower transparency for ourselves and as members of society in order to make progress. If we are genuinely honest with ourselves and in our relationships, sharing the same or similar vision, we have the capacity to reach better outcomes at a more rapid pace.

In the end, transparency in management practices will serve all stakeholders. The more that such practices and policies become transparent, the better and more effectively they will serve their shareholders, customers, workforce, and even communities. Yet, despite this motivation, all stakeholders do not empower, or believe in, this movement. In fact, the opposite holds true in many organisations, with the result that non-transparency triggers huge hidden costs from wasted resources, finances, and time for all stakeholders – expenditures that many leadership teams might not be able to evaluate or recognise but that also limit the individual and organisational potential to outperform. Nevertheless, hidden or not, recognised or ignored, this cost is one that all of society continues to pay.

But it does not need to be this way. With genuine leadership, we can accelerate this transformation for the benefit of everyone involved.

A Practical Scenario Simplifies the Lesson

Consider this example. Let's say, you, as a manager or recruiter, hired a person either from within the company or from an external source, sincerely believing that this person would perform well. However, it soon becomes obvious that you made a bad choice in hiring this individual. Initially, because you said "yes," it now becomes even more difficult to say "no" and to admit that you made a bad decision. Naturally, it is not easy for many people to accept that they made an error and – worse – by declaring that truth, potentially expose their faults and possibly place themselves personally at risk. Faced with this situation, the majority of people are likely to ignore the situation and hope that this bad choice will somehow disappear. But until, and unless, that happens, this mistake will continue to cause collateral damage in the organisation because you are afraid or uneasy about saying "no," even if it is to the detriment of company performance, just to save face.

But company performance is a very relative term that needs a contextual consideration. Although performance of 3%-5% growth might be acceptable to many organisations today, it is inadequate when the leadership team expects the organisation, and the workforce, to outperform. When almost everything becomes mediocre in the work environment, it becomes very difficult to envision how outperformance would taste. Consequently, management does not even attempt to change. Why bother, since everyone appears to accept mediocre results?

But let's think for a moment about what you have just done with that bad choice.

By not being transparent first with yourself and then with your actions, you become the reason for a certain amount of unnecessary inefficiency, wasted resources, and unspoken collateral damage for your organisation. Eventually, your leadership team, colleagues, shareholders, suppliers, clients, state, and even the community will pick up the bill for that negative result. Although no one will actually hand you the bill, payment is unspoken, unrecorded, and invisible – and you are not held accountable for your irresponsible behaviour.

Nonaction Is No Longer an Acceptable Answer

In light of this situation facing many organisations, the big question is whether we should continue to allow this kind of non-transparency. Instead, should we be proactive and use all the tools and approaches in our possession to stop the bleeding away of time and money? Wouldn't that make sense? Of course, but before we attempt to change the world around us, it is important to take a deeper look into why the status quo has such power. Consider:

- Why do shareholders not demand that leadership implement change in order to gain a better return on their invested capital?
- Why is management unwilling to invest in tools and approaches that will bring more transparency into their practices, along with the potential for more rewards?
- Why do governments discourage more transparency as a rule in organisations by adding more bureaucracy through "check-boxes" for better resource allocation?

The answers to these questions can provide enlightenment and a faster road to progress. For one thing, changing the status quo requires energy and will power, which must be gathered, nurtured, and shared. It's far easier to let "sleeping dogs lie" and leave the responsibility to someone else.

But whether leaders, organisations, or governments continue to resist the movement, technology is accelerating the transformation to transparency in unprecedented ways. Change is inevitable and will eventually overcome resistance. The best action for employees and their leadership teams to take is to get on board now and prepare the organisation for that transformation.

Saying "no" to mediocre results, leadership, or individuals is a good first step for all stakeholders and offers the promise of better outcomes. Saying "no" to bad practices and policies cultivates transformation. Saying "no" to mediocracy in the organisations you invest in, lead, or work in, while focusing on how you can outperform, is the clearest route for positive outcomes in the long run.

CHAPTER 8

RULE 2 - EMPOWER LEADERSHIP ACCOUNTABILITY IN EVERYONE

Why We Need Talented People to Identify Talented People

If you want talented people in your organisation, make sure that you have talented people to recognise and select them. Of the many key strategies for success that leadership should employ is the need to focus on encouraging the most talented people in the company to help find and hire the most talented people. As Arthur Conan Doyle once said, "Mediocrity knows nothing higher than itself…" That said, there is no point in hoping that the organisation can get the results for which it is striving if it uses not-so-talented people to pick so-called talented people! They would not recognise the talent!

This issue is not about junior or senior hiring. Rather, it is a question of organisational culture and has more repercussions to the entire business of an organisation than just simply to the hiring process. It speaks to wasted time and resources (both human and financial), lost productivity, errors, and other negative results.

Misunderstanding Clouds the Issue

Many organisations, at the very best, arbitrarily define a select group of employees as their key talent – the producers, the up-and-coming leaders. However, the question is not who has talent. Everybody does! The real question to ask is how to unlock and leverage the talent in every employee, as well as the candidates who want to join the organisation. By doing so, the majority of the workforce will have the ability to power the business in whatever direction mandated by leadership. The ultimate aim of any organisation should be to hire and continue to engage the right talent who willingly aligns with its business goals.

Practical Steps Save Time and Resources

So, what can leadership do?

1. As a start, simply stop spending money on pushing and pulling people to do a job – especially when it is apparent that such individuals are not engaged, are underperforming, and drag down the unit's success.

2. In addition, start investing in tools and approaches to help identify, engage, and retain the right talent within or outside the organisation who can grow the company in the most efficient and productive manner possible. For example, if the company has implemented a referral system, ensure that employees do not simply refer "a

friend" for an open position, but refer "a friend who has the skills and expertise the company needs."

3. Further, when economic conditions result in a low supply of desired talent, continue to be selective. Resist the urge to simply hire a body to fill a vacancy.

4. And finally, take the time to team build, engage in meaningful dialogue, listen to what employees are saying (especially what they are not saying), and train managers to "know" their staff. Most important, not only train the existing talented individuals to recognise the talent needed by the company, but also encourage them to reach their own potential through self-awareness tools and strategies.

The bottom line is simply this: Stop arbitrarily picking people and start knowing who can truly drive your business at all levels, organisation, division, function, group, and team if you want to truly outperform. Untap the hidden talent in your organisation and move forward, as an aligned team, to reach optimal results.

CHAPTER 9

RULE 3 - HELP YOUR EMPLOYEES TO LEARN MORE ABOUT THEMSELVES

Why Helping Your Employees to Learn More About Themselves Is a Better Solution to Increase and Sustain True Engagement in Your Organisation

Self-aware employees + Clear company goals = Outperforming organisation

Many organisations waste so much money and resources on hiring, developing, retaining, and rewarding "the wrong people." The outcome of these efforts has a huge impact on company results, be it profitability or productivity. Jacob Morgan, in his Harvard Business Review article,[21] provides compelling data and evidence of a strong correlation between company performance and employee experience. In his opinion, "most initiatives amount to an adrenaline shot. A perk is introduced …. over time the effect wears off." His study illustrates that "there is a significant return to

---

[21] "Why the Millions We Spend on Employee Engagement Buy Us So Little" (March 10, 2017).

organisations that focus on employee experience over the long term, not just engagement in the here and now."

That said, it is important to recognise that employee experience can mean different things to different people. So, we have to be careful when we use the term "employee experience/engagement." The focus should be on the issue of "employee vs. employer" alignment if our true intention is to significantly increase organisational performance.

Employee vs. employer alignment has two basic rules:

1) Ensure that employees are actually aligned with themselves (i.e., are self-aware).
2) With evidence of the first rule in hand, ensure that employees are willing to align with your company's goals.

If these rules are not validated within your organisation, you are wasting valuable resources on costly incentive programmes that might only bring incremental organisational improvement.

How Do You Know People Are Aligned With Themselves?

Obviously, personal alignment/self-awareness is not an easy task, prompting numerous perspectives, thoughts, and insights on the issue. Consequently, there are multiple ways that individuals can reach their destination. Although some will take longer than others, any effort is positive if it helps one to learn more about oneself. After all, a person who remains self-ignorant is not only a danger to that individual but also to society at large – a point that many people do not understand.

Of course, while we cannot expect every person to achieve self-awareness, anyone running a business should know whether the people who are working with them are self-aware. Otherwise, managers simply dwell in a land of wishful thinking, hoping that things will turn out well. In fact, they:

- Hire people and say, hopefully we made a good hire!
- Reward people and say, hopefully they will not leave!
- Train people and say, hopefully they have learned something!
- Promote people to leadership roles and say, hopefully they will lead!

You must do better than that when you run a business. You need to know if employees and colleagues know their strengths and weaknesses, have certain values, think about their future and actively plan for it, want to contribute, have a personal mission, are compassionate about others, and so on. You also should know whether those personal needs and interest are compatible with your company.

Employees and colleagues who have not thought about or are not even thinking about any of these factors are unlikely to contribute to the success of your company. Instead, they will be passive contributors who aim for the bare minimum. Regardless of whatever reward programme you deploy, you will not – and cannot – outperform in the marketplace with individuals who only make the bare minimum of effort. You will continue to waste value and resources for all stakeholders, including those passive contributors.

How Do You Align People vs. Your Company?

Conventional wisdom simply assumes that employees should follow employers' goals if they expect to earn rewards for whatever role they undertake. This wisdom also assumes that the source of the alignment should come from the employer.

In reality, it should come from both parties, as a one-dimensional effort does not work – or, at the very least, does not work well. Consider: Would you like to be with people whom you know are indifferent to your presence? Would you enjoy forcing people to behave in a certain way solely due to the influence of your money and the rewards you can offer? These scenarios will not result in positive outcomes over the long-term and will not provide a foundation for outperformance.

What Can You Do Now?

The more that employees are aware of their capabilities and wants, and the more that they align with a company's business requirements (technical and cultural), such companies should outperform the competition. The issue is not whether people like the office environment or their boss, for example – the so-called "employee engagement/experience" per say. The right question to ask is whether employees "know" their capabilities and, thereafter, whether they "like" and "know" what they "want" to do in life. The accompanying question to ask is whether those capabilities and wants match organisational goals.

Sincerely, if you really love what you do and you have all it takes to achieve something, do you really care where you work? Think of those people engaged in start-up companies who are enthusiastic about what they do in spite of frequently working in miserable conditions, including garages, rundown offices, and the like. They possess creativity, passion, dedication, and ambition among many other things. Are they disengaged? Absolutely not.

As a first step toward moving your organisation on the road to alignment, obtain a data-driven assessment of what is actually happening in your organisation. Discover what percentage of your employees actually "know" what they "want to do" in life and are aligned with what your business wants to achieve. With a clear idea of the situation, think about how you can improve your current state. Start having internal conversations around these questions if you truly want to outperform. The alternative, if you are satisfied with the status quo, is to sit passively and wait for your turn the next time a self-ignorant person tells you what to do.

What If Every Employee Had a Talent Agent?

Everyone knows that talented employees can make or break a business. But nurturing that talent is not so commonplace, though it should be standard practice.

The entertainment industry is familiar with the concept of a talent agent, the person who not only finds promising jobs for clients, but also defends, supports, and promotes their interests. Sometimes, the position responsibilities overlap with that of a client's manager, the person who oversees the client's daily business affairs. But beyond those tasks, the talent agent/manager advises and counsels the individual on professional matters, long-term plans, and personal decisions that may affect the person's career.

My son is a lawyer specialising in intellectual property, with a focus on the media and entertainment industry. His passion for the sector, even without possessing the law degree, already positions him as a young authority in whatever aspect touches the industry. For example, without hesitation, he can tell you which movie was produced, directed, financed, and distributed by whom – not to mention naming the actors who have appeared in movies for at least the last 20 to 30 years, listing the movies that will be released in the next two years, and which ones are more likely to succeed.

On a recent visit home, our family got together to enjoy our favourite pastime – watching a good movie – which he obviously selected! Over the years, we had established an informal ongoing discussion about actors, singers, directors, distributors, and screen writers, speculating as to why some became very successful while others did not. In the end, we always concluded that the number one reason for failure or lacklustre results was simple: Agents did not guide these people well, perhaps choosing the wrong song to sing or play, the wrong role or screenplay to act in, or partnering with the wrong director. Consequently, as so often happens, even if a person is very talented, passionate, skilled, and knowledgeable, without expert guidance (and, of course, luck), the chance of success is low.

The Need for Talent Agents in the Business World

If this concept of talent agents was applied to the corporate arena, the impact would prove advantageous for both the employer and employee, as well as shareholders. The reality of the modern workplace is that the majority of employees navigate their careers without well-thought-out guidance or a plan individualised for their needs and desires. Although many organisations invest in "career development," the effort is mostly generic, with the needs of the company taking priority. Deadlines are pending, clients are demanding, and employees are overworked, leaving little time to conduct a true focus on the employee's performance (or, lack of it). Often, managers' needs are first and foremost, with managers relying on subordinate performance to reflect well on their own careers, pushing them further up the corporate ladder.

The role of manager, whether in a profit or non-profit environment, has eroded in recent years. Its original function implied that the person was responsible for taking care of people in the manager's department. In a way, a manager's job was to act like a talent agent for subordinates, ensuring that employees performed a role best-suited for their individual success, as well as that of the organisation to optimise performance. Today's managers are often too busy to "manage" the overall function of the individual employee and simply "oversee" what the employee produces, whether a product or service. To regain a genuine manager-employee relationship, organisations must focus on increasing value for all stakeholders – shareholders, leadership, employees, and the community at large.

So, the question ultimately becomes: If every employee had a talent agent, would it significantly increase shareholder value, as well as value for all stakeholders, enough so to make a difference? I believe so. In fact, I believe that this approach could significantly and positively affect all stakeholders.

The Cost of Ignoring the Possibilities

But, the naysayers are already asking, at what price do we implement such a concept? Critics would be quick to argue that an organisation, especially a large global entity, could not possibly assign every employee a personal agent. As a compromise, they are likely to propose doing so only for the leadership team or high potentials in the organisation – the individuals who "matter."

So, my first question to those people would be, "how much do you think it is costing you now when you don't do it?" In reality, the price is colossal, eating away the organisation's profit margins, slowly but surely. Yet, that cost does not appear in the company income statement or balance sheet, so no one seems to care (or acknowledge). Unfortunately, if the truth were uncovered, shareholders would certainly sit up and take notice because the leadership team is not optimising their investment.

Wasted resources, in terms of time and money, are the result from hiring and retaining inefficient, ineffective, and underperforming employees. Continual training of new hires to replace the failed employees is an expensive proposition in terms of potential lost money, lagging productivity, the risk of low-quality products and services, customer dissatisfaction, peer resentment, and overworked high-performing employees. Along with myriad other negative repercussions, the bottom line is unnecessary damage that chips away from the company results more and more as time goes on.

Paths to Success

For the talent agent approach to be successful, managers need to be creative. Positive results do not come only by throwing money/carrots at people, such as generous reward programmes or budgets for training programmes that sound encouraging but only offer a general effort to boost employees' know-how and skills. Whatever steps are undertaken to promote the concept would not require large financial investments to nudge the mind and thinking of managers.

Instead, the approach demands some form of collaborative creative thinking – perhaps expanding the scope and responsibilities of mentorship or coaching programmes, or actually including the term "act like an agent" in the position description of managers. By giving managers more responsibility and accountability – and leadership must emphasise accountability – to help others to succeed, and not just themselves, the entire workforce could rise to the occasion.

Managers would benefit by asking their subordinates two questions: What do you want to do? What do you do well? The answers, when combined, should be able to point the employee's job duties in the right direction. It's simple common sense: By matching the individual employee with the task best-suited to that person's skills and know-how, everybody wins.

In fact, that process is what successful talent agents perform. They do not send actors to an orchestra's audition, or vice versa. The approach is not about simply getting the job done or achieving the company's goals. It's about getting the optimal job done with the focus on maximum value generation for all stakeholders while doing its best to meet the needs and desires of both the organisation and the individual. In the meantime, consumers and shareholders stand to gain as well, thereby boosting the organisation's long-term viability and performance sustainability.

CHAPTER 10

RULE 4 - TREAT YOUR EMPLOYEES LIKE YOUR BRAND

Why You Should Treat Your People Like Your Brand, Not Like Your Tangible Assets

To achieve the best of any situation, the activities of individuals who are motivated and invested in – not only in their own welfare, but also the organisation to which they belong – result in productivity, profitability, and effectiveness. Their performance excels, in both their personal and work lives, as they strive to be and do their best.

That said, not every individual or organisation succeeds in their endeavours. The number one reason, in fact, as to why many organisations fail to perform or outperform is due to the misalignment of business strategy and people's desires. When goals collide, the usual result is needless consumption and waste of personal and/or corporate resources. This outcome is particularly true when an employer recruits and hires candidates who do not fit the company's culture or brand. Managers must find and cultivate talented individuals who can take charge of their own growth while empowering others to achieve shared goals.

The Need: Accurate Data and Strong Leaders

The larger the percentage of misalignment between the two entities, the more challenging it becomes to attain optimal performance. It is that simple. But company leaders cannot simply reach an expected or desired outcome by an uninformed guess or assumption about the percentage of that alignment. The gap may be significant.

Sadly, many organisations do not even attempt to investigate this disparity and continue navigating their business as though flying a plane without a navigation system (GPS) in place. When, to no one's surprise, the plane crashes and everybody on board dies (or, the company fails and goes bankrupt), the business or the unit in question becomes obsolete. The few survivors typically conceive another so-called stellar strategy and repeat their mistakes over and over again, thereby wasting valuable resources, time, shareholder value – and, unfortunately, people! The individual victims become collateral damage, and nobody questions the cause.

This corporate behaviour is one of the most important arguments for having strong and capable leadership in our organisations. Solid leadership, from both the individual and organisational perspective, can help avoid or at least minimise such collateral damage. The word "leadership" is foremost about being "responsible" and "accountable" for things and for others, representing the number one reason why leadership exists – to take care of the business and, obviously, the people who make it happen. How can we even think of navigating our businesses in today's complex world without having a proper navigation system in place to inform our decisions?

The Answer: Appropriate Valuing of Employees

Consequently, managers need to stop guessing and start knowing and using tools that are critical to navigate the short-and long-term activities involved in their businesses. Although there are many tools available at our disposal, before jumping to conclusions as to which one(s) offer the most benefits, we need to step back and review a conventional misperception. The concept that employers should treat their employees as their most valuable asset is misleading and lacks serious reflection for the following reasons:

- People are not tangible assets, but are very intangible in many ways. Their value resides mostly in the intangible world, of which we have very limited control. Organisations can definitely contribute to increase the value of that intangible asset, but the only return is goodwill and nothing else.

- It is important to note that intangibles are called that because they are influenced by many more factors that are not necessarily in our control. That means their value is much more unstable than any other tangible assets. Of course, there are examples of tangible assets losing their value from factor beyond our control, such as business or political environment; however, when strictly compared, intangible assets are more unstable.

How can we then counter this instability and unknown? Treating your people with the same importance and respect as the company brand may represent an excellent starting point. It allows a conceptual shift to something more stable, sustainable, and strategic. "Branding," as a marketing practice, creates a name, symbol, or design that identifies and differentiates the company's products or services from that of competitors. Employees, as a form of company brand, should reflect the business by being engaged, motivated, positive, committed, and personal leaders. That is the brand that employers should embrace and support.

The Possibility: Success and Growth

That said, the idea of treating employees in the same way as one does a company brand or image requires care. Managers cannot simply say, "from now on, we are going to treat our people with the same importance as our brand." That would be a serious and damaging mistake. We have to first "know," rather than "assume," what percentage of our people are, in fact, aligned with the company's strategy to assess the potential of the employee brand to positively contribute to company goals.

The most significant trouble between employers and employees is that organisations do not take the time to evaluate, in an honest fashion on both sides, the compatibility between the two. Without that assessment, the concept of an employee brand will fail, as neither party is pen about their needs and desires. It is a shallow trade: work for money, without acknowledgement of any commitment to mutual growth.

But with genuine information, managers can strive to achieve better alignment to support this new thinking and vision for the business. The key is to only hire those individuals who fit the brand, who believe in the company's overall goals, and who truly represent the organisation in its best light to the public and its clients. Leadership should invest in programmes that facilitate employee self-discovery to attain sustainable growth and better resource allocation. In the end, what we really want to achieve needs to focus only on best outcomes – for both the business and individuals – and not settle for anything less than that.

CHAPTER 11

RULE 5 - IT IS ABOUT ALL EMPLOYEES, NOT JUST THE YOUNG AND UPCOMING!

Leveraging the Generational Potential to Accelerate Growth in All Economies

When it comes to economic progress, both developed and emerging market economies possess tremendous opportunities to accelerate growth for a number of reasons. If businesses and governments start recognising these opportunities and invest accordingly, the potential for growth will likely be unprecedented.

Key dissimilarities define both economies, and they face challenges in different ways. At the same time, some of these challenges also represent opportunities. For example, in emerging markets:

- Individuals are generally more open to change, willing to attempt new approaches, and not afraid of taking risks because they are obliged to grow faster to catch up with the rest of the world.

- This characteristic, in return, forces individuals to be more creative and easily accept change because they recognise that the problems they face can only be overcome by solutions that require innovative thinking and quicker adaptation to change. After all, they have been the champions of creativity thanks to the continuous daily pressure for survival and a hunger to improve their current state.

On the other hand, in developed markets:

- Individuals face tremendous pressure to keep what they have "built." They are generally more risk-averse because they seek answers/solutions to maintain what they "have."

- While this characteristic also forces individuals to be more creative, it does not necessarily put them at ease with change. After all, they believe that the problems they face should be overcome by incremental change and, consequently, do not see the need for drastic transformation.

The Extra Challenge for Emerging Economies

Putting aside these differences, the playing field becomes nearly equal. The proclaimed advantage of low-cost labour in emerging markets is an archaic thought; no nation will win that race because there is no winner in the long run. Cheap labour is generally unskilled and likely to focus on products and services that are mass produced. The quicker that emerging markets realise this fact, the sooner they will start to build economies that are much more sustainable over time. Price competition at a national level will only result, ultimately, in despair and deception, even though people experience an uptick in their overall income level in the short to mid-term.

In addition, emerging markets face another dilemma. Investment in automation and robotisation of labour work have been high in emerging markets in recent years. Consider China. Its recent five-year plan promotes the usage of industrial automation, with robots and computer numerical controller (CNC) machine tools identified as important areas for development.[22] The Chinese government stepped up its investment in training and developing professionals for the robotics industry, recognising that robots can help the manufacturing sector improve quality and efficiency, while reducing waste. As an example of the investments, a robot industrial complex is under construction in the Liaoning province; it was expected to generate revenues of US$8 billion for robots and other automation equipment by 2017. Coming years may witness a trend that is quite different and not so familiar in terms of labour force transformation in emerging markets. For example, consider these questions:

- What will happen to people who are under-educated, self-ignorant, and unskilled if automation and robotisation will not allow them to contribute as they have in emerging markets over the last 20 years?

---

[22] Christoffer Enemaerke, "Global Megatrends: Automation in Emerging Markets," RBC Global Asset Management (2014).

- What will happen to those people who enjoyed an uptick in overall income by moving to large cities and working in low-level jobs, but now lack the same opportunity?

The key success factor for the upcoming transformation is investment in education, learning, and training – three very different things. Education relates to the state in many of the markets; learning relates to the individual; and training relates to corporations. The quality of these three key ingredients of success will solely depend on governments' ability to stay up-to-date, the individual's ability to be more self-aware, and corporations' ability to be, at last, "truthfully" socially responsible.

The question of which population or employee segment in which to invest in order to grow the economy or business requires a crystal-clear understanding. Without that comprehension, a misunderstanding of this question may not only lead many nations and corporations into the dark for decades, but also potentially become a huge bill we will all have to pay. For example, if by ignorance, a nation or business leadership fails to invest in upgrading the knowledge of the elderly population or a specific employee segment, the nation or corporation in question will most likely perish. It is crucial to emphasise the importance of this understanding across all our nations and corporations.

As life spans continue to lengthen, society has an obligation to retain people in the workforce to ensure more continuity of contribution. However, a longer period of contribution does not necessarily mean forcing people to stagnate in the same job or career for another 20 or 30 years. New approaches and technologies can empower people and keep them as productive citizens as long as possible, while maintaining their interest and desire to contribute.

Identifying Two Key Employee Segments

The younger generation has a role to play in moving both developed and emerging markets forward through their view of the employee-employer relationship. Across developed and emerging markets, according to the 2016 Deloitte Millennial Survey, "millennials feel that most businesses have no ambition beyond profit. ... Millennials often put their personal values ahead of organisational goals." When asked to cite the values that support long-term business success, millennials overall replied:

- Employee satisfaction, loyalty, fair treatment (26%)

- Ethics, trust, integrity, honesty (25%)

- Customer care, focus (19%)

According to the survey, millennials in emerging markets are the least loyal to their current employers. When asked whether they expect to leave their organisation in the next five years, for example, 82% of millennials in Peru agreed, 76% in South Africa and India, and 74% in South Korea – compared to 64% in the US and 52% in Japan.

But millennials are not the only segment of the population that bears watching – and tapping. Retired (or retiring) individuals often represent an unexploited resource in many markets, with few organisations viewing them as a potential source of growth and innovation. Unfortunately, the term "retirement" does not connote an immediately accessible productive resource, which presents a number of issues:

- A very valuable experienced pool of talent is untapped and remains idle until it perishes.

- Viewing something as a cost instead of an asset leads to decisions that are not necessarily value driven.

- Wisdom, a most valued virtue, is not shared and disseminated with the rest of the population as it should be. Consequently, younger generations continue to make avoidable mistakes, triggering further persistent costs to society at large.

Bridging the Generations

But the situation does not have to remain this way. We can create a brand-new, value-oriented employee generation by facilitating a process and deploying a technology to bridge the experience, knowledge, and wisdom of the retired population with a younger generation who possess authentic inclinations. That untapped value can prove simultaneously beneficial not only to individuals, but also communities, organisations, and nations.

The key opportunity for all markets is to rapidly recognise the potential in all segments of the working population and facilitate the empowerment process for every citizen. That is the only sustainable growth model that can prevail in the long term. With the help of technology and novel approaches, we could enable this process even at a national level, helping countries to accelerate growth in all markets.

Finding and Empowering the Untapped Employee Potential

Without the efforts of your employees, working in harmony with leadership, an organisation is not likely to achieve long-term success. If employees are not aligned with the company's strategy, they may be busily working while merely spinning their wheels. In fact, rather than truly contributing to the company's performance, they may be steering it down the wrong road.

A report by Gallup[23] cites a discouraging estimate about employees in the US: The cost of poor management and lost productivity from employees who are not engaged or actively disengaged is between US$960 billion and US$1.2 trillion per year. In addition, large organisations spend tens of thousands of hours and tens of millions of dollars on activities that not only do not work, but also drive out top talent. What organisation can afford to waste such significant resources in terms of time, talent, opportunity, and money?

Leadership needs to create a clear direction for employees, encouraging their genuine engagement and providing structured guidance to willfully align with company strategy, with all parties striving toward mutually satisfying outcome. But how best to achieve this optimal state?

---

[23] "Re-Engineering Performance Management," authored by Ben Wigert and Jim Harter (2017).

Defining the Hidden Treasure

Many organisations ignore, or perhaps they do not bother to explore, two huge sources of employee potential with the ability to boost the company's profitability and sustainable growth agenda:

1. The first group is the "passively employed" population within their workforce (the forgotten talent). Such individuals are employed, as defined by traditional means, but actually perform just acceptable work within the organisation. Totally capable people, they possess their own convictions, passions, values, and meaning in life. But the company does not use them to their fullest capacity, not investing in them, and blocking their growth, because managers do not really explore these people and what they can offer. In fact, most leaders do not know how to extract the rich potential of these people in ways that could benefit all stakeholders. In effect, the "passively employed" are simply disengaged workers doing a satisfactory job.

2. The second group represents employees who perform good, adequate work, but who are not identifiable "high-potentials" in tune with the company's strategic goals. Acknowledged by their managers as being dependable, reliable, and effective employees, nevertheless, they do not share the vision (or, perhaps even truly acknowledge) where the company is heading and what it expects long-term in exchange for paying their salary. Managers typically

breathe a sigh of relief to have such good employees in their unit. But such individuals, too, are simply disengaged workers doing a decent job.

By not encouraging these employees to do what they do best in the most effective and productive way, companies neglect the welfare of these promising individuals. An unfortunate comparison is to consider such individuals as a farm field lying unused, dusty, dry, useless, and lifeless. But if fertilised and nurtured, the field can produce ripe, healthy, and nutritious food products that will sustain others for years to come. The same concept applies to employees who merely do an adequate, maybe even excellent, job, but have nothing to show for it other than good ratings and monetary rewards.

To make a sincere effort to uncover the potential of these individuals, who hold so much possibility, managers need to ask them:

- Are you able to live by your values in our organisation and are you satisfied with your overall efforts?
- Does your job reflect your passion, desire, and need for meaningful purpose?
- Do you believe that your mission matches that of the organisation?
- Do you care?

By identifying the individuals in these two groups, and nurturing their growth, leadership stands an excellent chance of accelerating where it needs to go in terms of profitability, sustainability, community involvement, and public image.

Identifying and Refining the Hidden Treasure

In most organisations, naturally, the leadership team is busy focusing on the overall company-wide picture and how it relates to the outside world, leaving managers to handle the day-to-day affairs of the business. Managers and supervisors shuffle mounds of administrative work, oversee employee activity, and solve daily problems, without having the quiet time to consider each individual subordinate and how that person fits into the overall organisational structure. At the bottom of the hierarchy, overworked employees complete their assigned tasks, with some more motivated than others.

With everyone concentrating on the demands of the workday, how can leadership and managers find the time to mine their employee resources and find the hidden gems – the untapped and productive employees who can help them truly move forward?

First and foremost, the leadership team must commit to caring for the welfare of all stakeholders and create a culture that will strive to align the majority of their workforce (ideally, all) with the company's short- and long-term goals. In addition, leadership must hold managers accountable for genuinely getting to know their subordinates: their pluses and minuses, skills and know-how, capabilities and at most personal goals. But to support this extra effort, leadership must provide managers with the time and the tools to achieve this goal without overburdening them with administrative bureaucracy.

With leadership backing their efforts, managers might consider the following practical steps to make a genuine effort to know their employees:

1. Treat each employee as a new hire. In other words, review the individual's résumé and credentials on an ongoing basis. Consider whether the person is under- or over-qualified for what the person does every day, as well as whether there are unused skills and interests that can be brought to bear on the job.

2. Conduct effective, efficient, practical, well-understood, and accepted performance appraisals. The Gallup report cites only 14% of employees strongly agreeing that their performance reviews inspire them to improve. Their aversion to traditional performance reviews are strongly tied to five primary psychological obstacles: infrequent feedback, lack of clarity, manager bias, adverse reactions to evaluation and feedback, and too much focus on pay incentives.

3. Hold ongoing mentor discussions. Employees today want a mentor who can talk to them, on an ongoing basis, about what the employee is doing, how well the employee is doing, how the employee fits into the company strategy, and, ultimately, what the employee wants to do. Continuous and engaging one-on-one discussions can go a long way toward inviting confidences, boosting credibility, and ensuring that employees understand their contribution.

4. Conduct focus groups to discuss overall strategy and the direction in which the organisation is headed. Ask for employee input and ideas and take note of which employees are creative and engaged.

5. Provide employees and managers with voluntary self-assessment tools. Although not all people have the time or interest in finding out more about themselves, they should be encouraged to do so. The more a person achieves self-awareness, the more they are able to contribute positively to their lives, their work unit, their employer, their family, and their community.

Making the Right Choice

In today's modern competitive world, it is too risky for leadership to ignore these two significant under-used segments of the workforce. Managers should not lightly dismiss such wasted resources of time and money when small steps – costing little in the overall scheme of things – can boost an organisation's long-term success and standing in the public eye. The choice is simple: surge forward, confident that the majority of the employee base is aligned with the corporate strategy, or shuffle along, reporting mediocre results through the efforts of a semi-engaged workforce.

CHAPTER 12

RULE 6 - FOCUS ON GENERATING VALUE FOR ALL STAKEHOLDERS

Why Generating Value for All Stakeholders Makes Business Sense

The most productive, successful organisations ensure that all stakeholders (management, employees, shareholders, customers/clients) gain some form of value for their participation in the enterprise. Without a positive return – be it in job security, profits and revenues, productivity – the parties would turn their time, talents, and attention elsewhere.

What Each Stakeholder Wants

Each stakeholder in an enterprise has desires and needs that must be met for the organisation to move forward, to thrive, and to survive in the global marketplace. If the company is fortunate, those desires and needs overlap to an extent that encourages cooperation and shared effort toward achieving results.

The leadership team wants the company to produce market results that earn a strong place among its competitors and peers. To reach this point, management expects employees to be innovative, highly productive, and efficient. By providing excellent products and/or services in the market, the company gains a positive public image, which, together, bring management their desired financial rewards, perquisites, and status.

In return for their efforts and labour, employees want competitive compensation and benefits, work-life balance, feedback and communication, and an understanding of where they fit in the workings of the operation. Employees also want to know that their effort makes a difference, so that they can leave the job satisfied at the end of their work day. Security, both present and future, is also desirable to a reasonable extent.

Shareholders spend money on corporate stock and expect a profitable return on that investment. They also want leadership teams who act with integrity, avoiding legal problems that could damage the company's standing in the community and adversely affect their investment returns. Shareholders also want communication from leadership on the state of the organisation's financial standing and future plans.

And finally, customers/clients want dependable, high-quality goods and services. They also require excellent customer service, with intelligent, knowledgeable, and trained employees having the authority to effectively address any problems or difficulties.

What Happens If They Do Not Get What They Want

If the different categories of stakeholders do not receive the value they legitimately expect, the consequences for the company's long-term viability may be grim. Typical scenarios, when the company fails to produce desired results, might include the following:

- Leadership may decide to cut back on resources, lay off nonessential employees, reduce or eliminate bonuses, freeze salaries, eliminate training programmes, curtail business travel, reduce research efforts, and take other actions that can eventually doom the company to stagnation.
- Employees are likely to lose their jobs; morale will drop; and employees will become disengaged and, potentially, careless, leading to poor product quality and lower profits.
- Shareholders will see stock value decline and capital gains drop, prompting them to sell their stock and invest elsewhere. In addition, they may express uncertainty and dissatisfaction about the company, thereby damaging the company's already spotty public image.
- Customers/clients, unhappy with poor quality and customer service, will take their business to the competition, reducing the enterprise's market share and revenues.

Some, all, or even more negative results can potentially occur, depending on a number of factors. If leadership is strong and willing to make an effort to engage employees in their shared dilemma, together, they may correct the company's downward spiral.

The Road to Value: Aligned Employees

That joint effort is the key to ensuring that all parties gain some form of value for their participation and investment in the company. Leadership must possess focused goals and a clear strategy first, before making the extra effort to get employees on their side. After all, having a straightforward goal, a generous budget, and skilled leadership may still not guarantee success without the support of the underlying force that drives the organisation: its workforce.

Employees, at least the majority of them, must align with leadership's desires, while ascertaining that their own needs are met. If the employee base is disengaged, if they feel unrecognised and neglected, and if they feel undervalued, they will not truly care what management wants. In fact, they may not even know what their work efforts are striving towards.

The road to that joint effort of successful cooperation begins with knowledge and information, regarding whether employees are a "fit" with the company's culture, as well as with their present occupation. Without that awareness, employees will come to work, perform a less-than-stellar job, and produce inferior results. But, possessing that knowledge, they will enter the office or factory or field site with motivation, energy, and the power to ensure that the company will generate value for all stakeholders.

SECTION 3:
ACCELERATING CHANGE TO ACHIEVE SUCCESS

CHAPTER 13

THE NEED FOR TECHNOLOGY TO ACCELERATE ORGANISATIONAL ALIGNMENT

In light of the prevalent disengagement found in many organisations, technology can be a great facilitator during the process of organisational alignment, accelerating the process significantly. However, technology alone is not yet sufficiently developed to assist us with this process and cannot replace – and should not remove the human element from – the efforts needed for organisational reflection or finding the true path to outperformance. One hopes an appropriate vehicle may exist in the future, providing stronger tools at our disposal to accelerate the process. For the moment, organisations must use what is available, while seeking and welcoming new approaches, improvements, and innovations every day.

Discovering the Right Tools

The most critical factor of technology is deciding what technology to use of the many methods available. All tout themselves to be the "holy grail" of the domain with which they are concerned, though few succeed to the degree they proclaim. Although technology attempts to resolve organisational issues through new tools, it cannot provide a lasting solution by offering the same old tools dressed in a shinier package. Radical ideas and brand-new approaches are necessary, ideas that support an organisation's actively taking charge and adjusting its own policies and practices with the help of technology. To prove effective, technology needs to empower leadership and the people from within the organisation, not from without; change must come with the help of technology, not made by technology.

For example, some believe that technological solutions should adapt to the way organisations operate today; that is, find an opening to penetrate the thinking of decision makers while they are doing what they are doing. What this approach represents is simply, "You can continue doing whatever you are doing today. While you are doing that, we can change things for your organisation." Unfortunately, this concept is simply charming, and people like charming things. Although attractive, such a concept misses the point, as the following example illustrates.

> The Dieting Dilemma: The charming concept may be the reason why many people with weight problems fall in love with seductive promises, despite the fact that the majority of specialised diets (whether or not they have nutritional value), fitness technology gadgets, and calorie-counting gizmos do not work because the product or service they buy has no lasting effects. What happens when dieters stop using the costly, specially prepared meals or find that counting calories or fat grams is too much of a bother (or they lose the shiny bit of technology that tracks their

progress – or lack of it)? Often, to the frustration of the dieter, the lost weight finds its way back home.

The Dieting Solution: At the core of the problem, the diets and technological "supports" do not empower their users to change their lifestyle or thought process or to reach for deeper knowledge about the true effects of what they are doing to their body by continuing to eat the same way every day. The advertisements, instead, encourage dieters to buy these products and services in perpetuity in order to reach and maintain their desired weight. They do not address the emotional, physical, or psychological reasons that underlie a dieter's gain/loss cycle and why they react to events in their life as they do. The technology to effectively and successfully address this issue must offer an approach to support organisational-awareness.

The Importance of Long-Term Benefits

Whatever issue technology is created to resolve (whether dieting, fitness, or other), the lasting impact of any such product or service, after discontinued use, can only come from a deeper acknowledgement and insight that transform one's thought process and opinions – which are, incidentally, two very different things. Although one's opinions may change over time, if people implement a conscious solid process as to how they perceive and reason in their minds, that process does not change often. However, many people become the victims of their long-established thought process, similar to the concept of self-prophecy. You are, after all, what you believe you are. If a person's thought process is inefficient and ineffective, thereby derailing that individual on the most critical decisions (such as livelihood), then it is imperative to take a good look and try to improve it in order to get back on track.

So, we need to use solutions that offer lasting, long-term benefits. The use of technology in organisational development with the purpose of outperformance, as well as compatibility among all stakeholders, is no exception. Consider this example from an employer's perspective, whereby the company is not going to find its next best talent and optimal candidate by:

- Asking tricky questions through an online survey

- Placing potential candidates into awkward situations to see how they react to a stressful environment in job interviews

- Painting a fake picture of the organisation to deceive candidates by making them believe that the company is a great place to work and they can progress in their careers, when, in fact, recruiters, personally, do not believe what they say

- Encouraging an external hiring process that is based on referrals without following up or checking (in other words, without the technology to manage such processes) how previous hires by that specific referrer might have performed historically

The Ultimate Goal

The bottom-line is simple: Management can deploy the right approaches for the right organisation in a timely manner based on technologies that bring transparency to management practices and communication, urge authenticity in people, and enable genuine human relationships within an organisation to outperform.

CHAPTER 14

A NEW DIAGNOSTIC TO HELP DISCOVER THE RIGHT TALENT

The corporate world spends billions of dollars and countless hours every year to recruit qualified employees, despite sometimes-disappointing success rates not only in hiring but also retaining key staff. According to research from Bersin by Deloitte, U.S. companies spend nearly three times the amount on recruiting efforts than they do on training per employee. The most mature recruiting organisations – defined as those considered strategic enablers of the business – spend US$6,465 per employee, on average, compared with only US$3,258 among organisations at the lowest level of maturity with reactive, tactical recruiting. But, according to the research, the investment is worth it: High-impact organisations have 40% lower new-hire turnover and can fill vacancies 20% faster.

With regards to timing, the 2016 MRINetwork Recruiter and Employer Sentiment Study offered another perspective. Candidates who rejected an offer pointed the finger at employer mistakes: Companies do not streamline their hiring practices to avoid their best candidates accepting another offer. Such companies also do not fully understand the target candidates' most important priorities, thereby losing them to the competition. The report cited the time for extending job offers as three to six weeks from the candidate's first interview, a shift from one to four weeks reported in the second half of 2015.

Faced with increasing expenditures of time and money, which ultimately impact the company's bottom line, employers need proactive and efficient alternatives.

Technology As a Workable Solution

Overwhelmed by mountains of candidate submissions from unqualified people, as well as internal pressure to fill job vacancies, the result is not surprising: Time is wasted, money is ill spent, and fallible decisions are made. This archaic process almost guarantees that people "who know people" are the only candidates being hired – whether or not the match is a good fit. Company policies that compensate for employee referrals encourage this outcome. Although employee references may (and, hopefully, should) prove advantageous, the risk of presenting individuals with the wrong skills and experience can lead to potential trouble down the road if the referral does not work out to the manager's expectations.

In a typical situation, while the hiring process drags on for weeks, some negative repercussions are possible.

> **The Problem: Traditional Recruiting Method**
>
> - Time spent in preparing the job search, writing advertisements, conducting candidate interviews, evaluating meeting results, making and negotiating offers, and filling out paperwork
>
> - Money wasted on advertisements, agency fees, external posting websites, new hire sign-on bonuses (if turnover is high), and relocating key candidates (if necessary)
>
> - Management dissatisfaction with loss of productivity, inefficient output, and decline in potential business and company performance when a job is vacant too long or another employee (unfamiliar with the job responsibilities and unhappy with an added workload) is temporarily filling in
>
> - Unqualified applicants responding to advertisements and overwhelming hard-pressed (and too few) HR staff who may make subjective judgment calls simply to fill another vacancy
>
> - Displeased shareholders if the overall performance of the company falls off

Algorithms, or formulas, that are capable of discovering the right talent amid overwhelming numbers of applicants can change that end result, potentially minimising the risk factors of employing the wrong person. After all, hiring is often a throw of the dice –and the employer-employee match may very well prove unprofitable and unproductive for either or both parties if not carried out in an objective, rational manner.

One promising solution to HR's dilemma is sparkChief™, an innovative diagnostic tool that analyses the background and potential of candidates, offering a genuine spark of hope for both job seekers and employers. The algorithm, on which the tool is based, encompasses a set of criteria to examine the underlying current understanding and status of a person's progress towards fulfilling his or her goals. More important, for a minimal fee, the system has the capability to match an individual with a hiring company in minutes, so that job seekers can receive job offers within 24 hours after inputting their information into sparkChief™'s database. Time and money well spent when one considers the wasteful extravagance of the traditional recruiting process.

Why the Algorithm Works

The science behind sparkChief™'s algorithms, called "advanced personal progress scanning" (APPS), separates the core factors that form the foundation of a candidate's career and aspirations. It quantitatively considers the individual's weaknesses, strengths, potentials, strategy, skills, goals, actions, and personal vision – resulting in a user-friendly model built upon the data captured by the software. The tool does not merely match similar words in a person's cv/resumé with a company's position description. Instead, it goes beyond a simplistic "search and find" function to analyse the person's experience and potentials. By comparing candidate results to detailed job profiles submitted by employers in a measurable, rather than subjective, manner, it enhances the ability of the typical recruiter to make optimal matches quickly and inexpensively.

sparkChief™'s algorithm may prove to be the solution that today's employers and job seekers need, transforming the recruiting process from a nightmare to a practical reality. When searching for key staff, corporations of all sizes, non-profit organisations, government institutions, and nongovernment organisations in different industries and world regions look for a certain kind of talent, actual experience, and specific skills. Recruiters attempt to fill vacancies, created by either new jobs or turnover when previous candidates fail to perform. Hiring the wrong person will only increase recruiting costs (to replace the unsuccessful employee) and training costs to bring the new employee up to speed. Consequently, if the right candidate is hired (with appropriate skills) the first time and recruiting costs lowered, training costs should be minimal, too, along with other benefits.

The Answer: sparkChief™

- Only qualified candidates are considered, as the system matches the appropriate individuals for the position, resulting in more time spent on the right people.

- Better focus is placed on suitable talent without "settling" for an unqualified candidate, simply to fill the vacancy.

- HR processes work with improved efficiency, bypassing the need to bring in more recruiting staff (who, in turn, would result in higher employee-related costs for compensation and benefits).

- The recruiting and hiring process demonstrates increased objectivity, measurability, reliability, and transparency – resulting in improved credibility to stakeholders.

- Less money is spent on advertisements, agency fees, and repetitive sign-on bonuses.

Businesses depend on finding the right person for the right job in the right place and at the right time. If successful, sparkChief™ opens the possibility of revolutionising the recruitment process by transforming traditional hiring and career planning into a scientific, efficient, and effective strategy.

- From the individual's perspective, having skills and a high potential without access to right opportunities is worthless.

sparkChief™ allows talent – often lost in the crowd, unknown and unrecognised – to come to the attention of employers. As it helps HR sift through thousands of candidate applications to find the best person who can make a positive contribution to the company's bottom line, sparkChief™ simultaneously advances the individual's career.

- From the company's perspective, finding the right talent can boost the success rate of the recruiting function, reduce employee-related costs, significantly improve business performance through hiring engaged and motivated employees, and boost the company's long-term viability in an ever-competitive marketplace.

sparkChief™'s diagnostic tool can sort the right candidates from the wrong ones, allowing a company to swiftly find the best candidate who matches – not merely comes close to – the specifications of the job posting.

Partnering to Reach the Same Goal

While the reasons for using such a tool are persuasive, particularly for job seekers, recruiters might very well balk at implementing such a system, viewing the technology as a threat to their own jobs. It is all about perspective. If the tool could result in better use of recruiting dollars, more efficient expenditure of time, and a cadre of qualified candidates, it can prove to be a win-win solution.

The human factor will always be a participant in the hiring process. The algorithm can only work if candidates provide accurate data and remain true to themselves about their skills and their requirements, and recruiters exercise discretion and judgment. As time goes on, with the expansion of sparkChief™'s client base, more and more employers will acknowledge the advantages of adding a quantitative method to their subjective recruiting process. Not only is it common sense, but it is also simply a matter of time.

CHAPTER 15

GETTING READY FOR THE FUTURE: THE ROADMAP

To help individuals address the need for lifelong learning, personal leadership, and self-awareness – and organisations, as well – the algorithm behind the sparkChief™ model incorporates specific criteria. Those factors, accompanied by honest input from the user, serve as a roadmap whereby a person can understand and determine the best fit for one's knowledge, talent, desires, and goals. This information can lead a person toward the right path – be it education, employment, or simply a fulfilling life.

The model considers four general stages of progress to move from thought and ideas to practical action.

1. The Roadmap: Enlightenment

Enlightenment conjures up the concepts of insight, awareness, wisdom, education, learning, and knowledge. This stage represents the initial steps that reveal the different aspects of the self – some of which may have been undiscovered and, therefore, untapped. It discusses an individual's values and purpose in life, along with a fair assessment of the abilities that a person can offer.

2. **The Roadmap: Validation**

Validation refers to checking or proving the validity or accuracy of something. This stage affirms the self-knowledge gathered, allowing the user to recognise and think about how one can build on that foundation to look toward a better, more meaningful future in practical terms.

3. **The Roadmap: Synthesising**

Synthesising involves combining a number of things or elements into a coherent whole to make something new and unique. This stage represents an exploration of the external environment, as well as the trends that influence our decisions. It helps us to understand the reality of the world around us and how we can work within the limitations of existing conditions to negotiate a path that will lead toward achievement of our goals.

4. **The Roadmap: Execution**

Execution, the final stage, refers to the actual carrying out or putting into effect a plan or course of action. With all the pertinent information in place – both internal and external factors – this phase sets achievable objectives that are concrete and reasonable, yet stretches a person's abilities to reach untapped potential. With these objectives in mind, the individual can make informed decisions to take action, placing control of one's life, as much as possible, in one's own hands.

The following case studies present practical examples of how employees can benefit from an honest self-assessment through the sparkChief™ tool.

Case Study 1: Steve – 30-year-old employee

The Context and the Issue

Steve, who lives in London, UK, started his career right after graduation from the university with an MBA degree. So far, he has been successful and earns a good salary in his second key role as a marketing manager for a multinational consumer goods company. Steve is about to start a new family with his girlfriend, whom he met through friends a couple of years ago. He has always achieved his objectives at work and, at times, even exceeded them. He gets along with his peers, as well as his boss, who describes Steve as a "high-potential" employee.

However, Steve is a bit concerned about his future. Although he enjoys his work, he also believes that he would not like to do the same thing for the rest of his career. According to his mentors, Steve needs to work his way through all the functions, regions, and a few business units to truly progress in his career. Lately, Steve has faced a challenging period as he wonders whether the consumer goods industry is the right sector in which to build a career. In addition, the buzz from his colleagues is that the sector is experiencing pressure to be more efficient and cost-conscious, with margins falling due to ever-increasing competitiveness in the global economy.

Although Steve has had many discussions and exchanges with close friends, his girlfriend, and parents, he senses that those conversations missed something more profound than their tactical suggestions. He feels he needs to go deeper on his own to bring together his ideas and thoughts, together with the advice he has received, in order to determine his next move before navigating further along his career path. After all, he hates the thought of finding himself unhappy and unsatisfied with his career choice at age 45 when it would likely be more challenging to make a change.

The New Approach

Steve decides to take the sparkChief Progress Scan to assess and conceive a plan for his future to enhance his career and develop himself as an individual, while inspiring others.

Based on the Progress Scan, which examines 14 critical factors for an individual, Steve came to a number of realisations. There are a few important factors to which he needs to pay closer attention to discover the most effective approach for him to progress forward.

- Discovery 1: Although Steve seems focused and has had a successful track record so far, he has never given thought to what truly drives him in life. He recognises that, at the bottom of his heart, he cares deeply about learning new things and applying knowledge for the benefit of other people.

- Discovery 2: Steve strong believes that without learning, one cannot be successful in life, especially with all the advancement taking place everywhere due to technology. He discovers that he has a particular interest in communications and how we use it to explain things to each other. Steve has been tinkering with his "pet project" to establish a blog focused solely on how people from different cultures define and use different means of communication to connect with each other. While he loves reading and learning about new subjects, Steve also loves writing. He realises that the reason he wanted to build his blog was to practice all these desires simultaneously.

Results

After extensive reflection and rigorous validation, backed by honest feedback from people whom he really cares for and respects, Steve decides to move into the media sector. He plans to become a content development and purchasing director in a leading publishing house in London.

Case Study 2: Bo – 45-year-old Human Resources executive

The Context and the Issue

Bo works at a leading international logistics firm, based in Singapore. She started her career in HR 20 years ago. While she has worked for many large multinationals, mostly in their regional operations in Asia Pacific, Bo has also lived and worked in New York as an expatriate for three years. She has a very global mindset and is considered to be one of the most influential HR executives in Singapore. During her time in HR, Bo's experience has touched on nearly all aspects of the field, including rewards, talent management, and international assignments. As a well-rounded HR executive, Bo is a frequent speaker at conferences and forums across the region.

Recently, her leadership team gave her a mandate to closely align her company business strategy with their workforce strategy. The leadership team wants Bo to move quickly on this project, encouraging her to be as open-minded as possible in terms of finding new approaches to allow the company to significantly improve its performance vs. that of its competitors. The latest engagement survey findings indicate that a majority of regional employees are satisfied with their leadership team, yet there seems to be a tendency to leave the company if another opportunity appears on their doorstep.

The company bases its current business strategy on a fast-track growth model that necessitates creativity in all functions, departments, and business units. The shareholders want to accelerate earnings and maximise their return on their invested capital. In addition, while market conditions have been deteriorating in some key markets, they are still relatively better than in other regions, considering what has been happening in Europe. The leadership, therefore, believes that the company needs a new approach to organise its business and empower its workforce to perform at an optimum level, thereby placing the company in a leading position among regional competitors.

Bo has been an advocate for change for a long time within the firm. However, as the situation seemed acceptable and margins were achieved, no one in the company dared to rock the boat – particularly in recent years when most sector companies faced turbulent times across the region. Bo is determined not to settle for a short-term solution or follow a traditional strategy that most companies follow – that is, go through a typical reorganisation process, eliminate excess capacity in the workforce, downgrade some roles to reduce workforce costs, load employees with more responsibility, and, ultimately, declare victory because the firm gained a couple of more points on their net operating income.

The New Approach

Bo decides to do something different, convincing the management team to address the root cause of their problems rather than the symptoms. She implements the sparkChief Progress model and scans the entire employee population to obtain a more truthful reading of the organisation. Although her strategy entails a risk, she is willing to take it despite the potential for unpleasant findings (transparent as they are). However, it will allow the firm to undertake a profoundly fresh start to develop and grow its potential and achieve unprecedented higher performance levels.

Based on the Progress Scan, which examines 14 critical factors for each employee, the leadership team came to a number of realisations. There are a few important factors regarding their current organisation that require immediate attention in order for the company to improve margins, ready the firm for accelerated growth, and benefit all stakeholders (shareholders, board members, management, and employees).

- Discovery 1: Bo discovers that almost 70% of employees do not share the company's mission. Although employees seem content with the leadership and perform reasonably according to set objectives, management never asked them if they shared or cared about the mission of the firm set forward by the leadership. The company modified its mission in recent years, but never validated it as to employees' beliefs. Management assumed that the new mission should, by default, be accepted by all employees. The mission statements appear in annual reports, are included on company intranets, and are displayed on corporate office walls. But the simple truth is that by not enlisting employee support, the company caused an unspoken misalignment at the foundational level within the organisation.

- Discovery 2: Bo, as a very seasoned HR professional, strongly believes that investment in training is a good thing, often proving itself worthwhile, and so encourages spending more training dollars on all employees. However, strangely enough, when recent engagement surveys asked why people would leave the firm, most employees responded, "for better career development opportunities." That response did not make sense for a company willing to invest in training to help employees better themselves at their job. Bo discovered that actually providing training to the misaligned employees resulted in a conventionally acceptable return, but never an outstanding outcome for "all employees."

Results

After extensive reflection and rigorous validation, backed by honest feedback from employees who truly shared, cared about, and were committed to the company strategy, the firm decided to only hire employees who love what they do and commit themselves to improve both company results and further their careers. The firm also plans to implement a new programme to transition employees to roles in which they would be more effective.

Following the Roadmap into the Future

Through the sparkChief™ model, individuals can undertake a journey of self-discovery that creates a personal portfolio of knowledge, talent, desires, and goals. With this self-awareness, an individual possesses a solid foundation on which to make major and minor decisions throughout every stage of the life cycle – whether it involves family life, community involvement, education, employment, or simply one's personal dreams. It serves as a vehicle through which an individual can evaluate whether personal goals are a fit for a course of study, career, or an employer's culture.

But to be proactive and move forward in life requires an understanding of a simple and basic truth: There can be no progression without first dealing with the root cause of a problem or condition. People need to take time and dive deep into themselves to explore what is possible and what is feasible – to step beyond a life of complacency and mediocrity to resolve whatever issues they may face. By shining light on the core of our identities – who we are, what we value, and of what we are capable – we are then able to lead a fulfilling life on our own terms.

However, some individuals persist in telling themselves that they are not capable of doing anything – a patently false statement, as everyone is capable of doing at least something. Every individual has a talent, a reason to be. The likelihood is that most people just do not know what that may be or perhaps lack support in discovering what it can be. Unfortunately, such people remain in the dark – sometimes for a long time, and, sadly, sometimes until the end of their lives.

This reservoir of untapped potential represents a significant waste. One should not doubt, but should, instead, seek guidance to fulfil one's capability and make a positive contribution to the world in which one lives.

CHAPTER 16

PRACTICAL STRATEGIES FOR FOLLOWING THE ROADMAP

The factors included in the sparkChief™ model lead an individual through a step-by-step examination of what lies at the core of a person's purpose in life. Through the stages of enlightenment, validation, synthesising, and execution, the user reaches a place that points toward a path filled with potential opportunity.

But the process requires a cautious approach for optimal results. The following discussion provides practical suggestions about what a person should expect when navigating through the sparkChief™ roadmap – or any other self-assessment tool.

Seven Key Points for Following the Roadmap

1.   Timing is, as always, important.

When faced with a major life decision, step back, take a deep breath, and consider all options before taking action. The choices involved at different stages can be overwhelming – finding a passion, choosing a course of study, advancing in a career, finding a life mate to start a family, starting a business, re-inventing oneself, thinking about volunteer efforts, and so on. At times, the decisions that one is pressured to make can coincide; for example, finding a life partner and seeking a new job. While the issues may differ, the end point is the same: find the best person or position or whatever that best suits your needs and desires.

2. Verify your core values thoroughly.

Possibly one of the most important criteria, one's core values lay the foundation for major life decisions. These choices can have a significant impact on a person's family, peer group, and others. Reflecting on core personal values should take as much time and effort as necessary to understand what makes you tick.

When doing so, consider whether the values you have stated are the ones in which you truly believe – or, whether they are values you are expected to uphold, as suggested by family members, peers, an employer or mentor, or society at large. The values should be a reflection of a genuine "you." Honesty, here, is essential.

3. Seek out objective feedback, even from people you do not appreciate.

When conducting a self-assessment, it is helpful to ask mentors for their suggestions and feedback, but take your own advice. After all, who knows you better than you do?

Mentors at different life stages – not only during a period of introspection – offer value if the relationship is based on true, independent, and authentic communication. Remember, mentors should be there to provide you with objective commentary. Although some feedback may not be positive, it should be constructive. If the mentorship is based on mutual interests, thereby lacking objectivity and honesty, then you are not talking to the right people.

Mentors are not the only source of guidance. People who "like" you, who share mutual respect and affection, are likely to offer positive feedback only. Those whom you may not appreciate – or get along with – may have a very different view of you, possibly one that is not 100% favourable. Recognising how they think about you, even though you do not agree with their perspective or opinions, can offer a decided advantage that may prompt you to reconsider your views on who you really are. It may prompt you to accept something negative about yourself that you may have been avoiding, thereby offering improvement and growth.

But remember, a different perspective is just another perspective, that's all. Acknowledgement does not mean acceptance. Once more, be honest.

4. *Take time to reflect. Do not rush to conclusions and follow the steps – don't skip!*

Unfortunately, the world we live in is all about shortcuts and instant gratification. Everyone seeks a shortcut to something, an easy way to achieve what we want without putting too much time and effort into it. But to become a mature individual and sustain fulfilment, it is far better to reach that goal through gaining a full awareness and authentic acceptance of whom you are – not the person whom a quick test assumes you to be. That is the only way to grow as a person.

Learning about oneself is not a process that should be rushed. When discovering different aspects about yourself that may have gone unrecognised and hidden – or, possibly, avoided – take time to think about the implications for your life and reflect on the possibilities they open up.

There is no off-the-shelf miraculous solution waiting at the end of the process. The roadmap works in two ways, by providing:

- A quick snapshot of where you are at this point in your life, and

- A mindset to explore your path to fulfilment.

The first point is a quick exercise, while the second one will involve time and effort to finalise. If you attempt to rush to conclusions about what you discover, without taking your time to think and reflect about each new finding (because you assume you already covered that criteria), you run the risk of bypassing the opportunity to make strategic, informed decisions. Doing so haphazardly will either cause you to waste time or misguide your direction.

5. Sleep on it, but don't wait too long.

Once you have gone through everything that the process of self-discovery entails, sleep on your reflections. Some thoughts change when the conscious mind stays away from them for a while; some do not. Stick with the ones that remain the same after careful reflection.

Although a person should not rush through the self-discovery journey, don't wait too long either. The quicker you start acknowledging the facts and making concrete plans to change or improve your life, the better your chances of achieving whatever you desire. Timing, as they say, is everything.

6. *Walk your talk and act accordingly.*

Thoughts without action are meaningless pipedreams. Once you complete the self-analysis, take steps to ensure that every resource at your disposal is geared toward meeting those objectives in the best way possible. Focus on your path, and avoid doing anything else that will waylay you – but be sure that your actions cause no harm. Navigate your way through life decisions with actions that serve to support your values.

7. *Don't limit yourself – revisit your interests.*

Sometimes people hesitate about which path to choose to reach their destination, forgetting that there are often many roads available. And, more important, those alternatives are likely to change as time goes on and new opportunities beckon. The only criterion that you should keep in the forefront of your thoughts is that whatever you choose to do should move you in the direction of your goals. Don't follow byways that veer off 10 degrees left or right. Keep your eyes glued to the end point.

That said, from time to time, revisit your initial interests to make sure that you still enjoy doing things that feel right for you. As time progresses, and you pass through different stages of the life cycle, so may your desires and goals change. Stay attuned to your true self and listen to your instincts if they signal a bend in the road.

CHAPTER 17

PRACTICAL EXAMPLES OF SELF-ASSESSMENT USERS

Self-assessment is not restricted to personal use. Beyond an individual's need to gain self-knowledge, the value of the process lies in its usefulness for people at different stages of their life – whether young students, employees, or job seekers. Further, an assessment offers organisations a practical and effective tool to boost their growth and financial viability through seeking and hiring the right individuals who can bring engagement, talent, expertise, and potential to support the company's strategic vision.

The following examples highlight the ways in which different categories of users can take advantage of a self-assessment process, for example, through the sparkChief™ application.

Users: Job Seekers (Employees Seeking New Opportunities, Untapped/Unemployed Persons)

The ideal way to deploy the proposed self-assessment tool for individuals seeking work is through the assistance of personal coaches. There are two components to the assessment process:

- A quick insight about where each employee/unemployed person stands against his or her personal development progress, which is facilitated through a mobile application that provides them with instant feedback on four key dimensions of their personal progress.

- A set of interviews to guide employees/unemployed persons in their efforts to further explore areas where they feel they need more clarification and validation; depending on the overall status of each individual's personal progress, coaches need approximately two to four hours to support each individual.

Once the validation phase is accomplished, personal coaches then guide each employee/unemployed person to collate the pieces through interviews and personal reflection time. The outcome of this phase, in terms of time for the individual, can vary from a few weeks to a few months, depending on the engagement level of each individual, time spent for personal exploration, and feedback from others. The overall time needed with a coach during this phase can be somewhere between two and three hours.

The final step involves making an action plan for each employee/unemployed person. Most often, individuals take the lead during this phase with periodic checks and meetings with personal coaches.

Any current employee, job seeker, or untapped person (a.k.a. unemployed) can use the assessment tool at any time in their career to assess and explore their potential or confirm the direction they have taken earlier in their career.

Users: Employers

The ideal way to deploy the proposed self-assessment tool in organisations is through the assistance of independent consultants. There are two components to the assessment process:

- A summary report about where the total employee population stands against company vision, objectives, and business strategy at a given time, which is facilitated through an aggregate analysis of employees' assessment results based on four key dimensions of their profile.

- A set of executive meetings to guide management in their efforts to further explore areas of compatibility between business goals and workforce needs, followed by discussions to further clarify or validate goals if necessary. Depending on the overall gaps uncovered, these meetings need approximately two to three hours to guide the management team.

Once the validation phase is accomplished, independent consultants then guide the management team to bring the pieces together through a series of senior-level interviews. The outcome of this phase, in terms of time for the individual, can vary from a few weeks to few months, depending on the engagement level of the leadership team and support from management. The overall time needed with senior leadership during this phase is somewhere between two to three hours.

The final step involves making an action plan for the organisation. Most often, leadership drives this phase with regular meetings with independent consultants.

Employers can deploy the assessment tool at any time in their organisations to assess and diagnose the gaps between business goals and workforce needs to accelerate significant growth or to confirm its strategic direction taken earlier.

Users: Recruiters

The ideal way to deploy the proposed self-assessment tool is with job applicants. There are two components to the assessment process:

- A quick scan about where each applicant stands against his or her personal development progress as an individual, which is facilitated through a mobile application that provides applicants with instant feedback on four key dimensions of their personal progress.

- A plot of applicant results against the recruiter's job profile criteria based on organisational requirements. Only applicants, based on the recruiter's definition, corresponding to the company and job profile, go forward to the next phase of the recruitment process.

Once the filtering process is accomplished, each applicant moves on to interviews and the validation period. The outcome of this phase, in terms of time for the applicant, can vary from a few weeks to a few months, depending on the flow of the hiring process by the recruiter. However, the overall time needed throughout the recruitment cycle drastically reduces as recruiters only focus on candidates with the highest compatibility.

The final step involves making an action plan to decide on the appropriate applicant and make the individual a job offer.

Any applicant can undergo an assessment at any time during the application process to determine the individual's potential and compatibility with the organisation.

Users: Human Resources During Reorganisation/Separation

The ideal way to deploy the proposed self-assessment tool is during any reorganisation effort. There are two components to the assessment process:

- A quick scan about where each member of a business line or function stands against his or her personal development progress as an individual, which is facilitated through a mobile application that provides individuals with instant feedback on four key dimensions of their personal progress.

- A plot of each employee in each business unit or function against the company's new organisation profile based on new business requirements. Only employees corresponding to new job profiles, based on the newly designed organisation structure, are eligible for positions within the business unit or function.

Once the streamlining process is accomplished, employees who remain move on to validation through interviews. The outcome of this phase, in terms of time for the employee, can vary from a few weeks to a few months, depending on the flow of the reorganisation efforts. However, the overall time needed throughout the reorganisation cycle drastically reduces as the leadership team only focuses on employees that indicate the highest compatibility.

Although all employees within the concerned business unit or function undergo the same assessment process, the results assess a percentage of employees who are not compatible with the new organisational strategy. HR personnel guide those individuals to move on to more compatible units or functions within the company, if possible. If there is no appropriate position within the company, independent coaches guide these employees toward the next steps to find opportunities outside the firm through additional interviews and personal reflection time.

The outcome of this phase, in terms of time for the employee, can vary from a few weeks to a few months, depending on the engagement level of each employee, time spent for personal exploration, and feedback from others. The overall time needed with a coach during this phase is somewhere between four and six hours.

Any employee can undergo assessment at any time during the reorganisation/separation process to determine the individual's potential and compatibility with the organisation.

Suggestions for Users in Obtaining Feedback During Self-Assessment

No matter the category – whether the user is an individual seeking self-knowledge or an organisation conducting an employee survey – the process of obtaining feedback becomes critical when conducting an honest self-assessment. Although we often wonder how others perceive us in our relations and interactions with them, we seldom ask for their honest feedback and opinions. Good family members, friends, and possibly colleagues might offer honest feedback from time to time. Parents usually do – without being asked!

When considering what people say about us – as individuals or entities – we might dismiss some comments. This reaction may occur, whether or not there is a bit of truth in the feedback we receive from those people who care about us. If those we query are honest, and truly care, it is important to listen to what they say, view it with integrity and an open mind, and decide whether or not it holds true for us. Obtaining such feedback is an essential factor in undergoing such a personal self-learning exercise.

Although the main purpose of feedback is validation, remember that you do not need validation from others – even persons to whom you are close – in order to know or decide what actions you should take in your life. That said, validation serves an important role in determining whether others have a drastically different view of oneself. Should that happen, at the very least, just acknowledging the difference is worthwhile. Without that awareness, a person can run the risk of self-prophecy, as many individuals do, believing things about themselves that are not true. Consider all the people you know who hold on to an image of themselves from, say childhood, an image that their parents imposed upon them – an image, in fact, that they have outgrown or have never really possessed.

When requesting feedback from others, always give them sufficient time to think, reflect, digest, and provide honest feedback. A week is an ideal period. Remind them not to take shortcuts in their responses, as half-baked feedback is worse than no feedback at all. Quick answers might derail you and waste your time. So, if they do not have time or the ability to focus on the process and offer thoughtful feedback, it is preferable to ask someone else.

Self-Assessment: A Matter of Privacy

Remember, as self-assessment is a private matter, a third party without any self-interest in the process is the best entity to sponsor and conduct the analysis. The results from the self-assessment should also be mobile. After all, you own the information and should oversee and possess that data.

If an employer, for example, offers the opportunity to conduct a self-assessment, make sure that you decide what parts to disclose to the employer, based on your self-assessment. The only information your employer needs to know about you is whether your individual profile fits with their business profile. That's all!

CONCLUSION AND FUTURE THOUGHTS

Keep Your Eyes on the Ball! But Which Ball?

Throughout my career, I have been part of diverse global leaderships teams and held various positions of responsibility. Many years ago, one of our business leaders, who was responsible for the unit, frequently advised us to "keep our eyes on the ball!" During almost every monthly financial call, and at the end of every call, he repeated these words. "Don't forget to keep your eyes on the ball!" Nobody thought to question him about what he really meant.

At the time, my assignment involved building a new global product line that would be managed in multiple locations. My participation in helping to launch this business successfully was critical for my career; I had to prove that not only could I do it, but also that I could do it with sustainable results. All I had on hand to initiate the project was a very good brand and, of course, an approved strategic decision supported by the global leadership to invest in this new business. From my perspective, "keeping my eyes on the ball" simply meant that I had to ensure that the business generated revenues and profits within the established timelines – or, my position and reputation would be in jeopardy. Hearing our global business leader repeating his phrase, mostly on the financial calls, I assume, looking back, that we all implicitly thought he was referring to the financial metrics and results that he expected.

A Conversation and Good Advice

After a few other calls, I believed there had to be more to what he was saying. Knowing how critical the project was to my career and the company's bottom line, I had to be certain that I knew what he expected from me. So, I asked, "What do you really mean by 'keep your eyes on the ball'? Financial results?" To that, he replied, "Listen Ali, what do you think is the most important ingredient of a successful business?" My immediate response was, "revenue growth and profitability." To which he responded, "Wrong. Revenue and profitability is the cause of something else."

Considering the scale of our client base at the time, whatever we introduced in the market would enable us to sell a few new products to generate some revenue. With that in mind, I tried again: "Well, what about scale?" He replied in the negative, adding, "The people whom you select to work with is the most important ingredient of any successful and sustainable business. You need to keep your eyes on your people all the time. The moment you stop doing that, you will start losing." He also offered this advice:

- Keep an eye on the people you hire.
- Keep an eye on the people you trust to give accountability to lead.
- Keep an eye on the people you promote.

- Keep an eye on the people you select to fill critical positions.
- Keep an eye on the people who behave wrongly to others.
- Keep an eye on the people whom you develop and prepare to grow the business for the future.

And finally, "As long as you do these things, you will not have to worry about anything else. Trust me!"

The Right Focus

Being young and naïve at the time, his advice prompted a mind-shift for me. Ever since, the only thing I focus on in a business is on people. Plain and simple.

After a few years working together, we all moved on to new roles. While he held several CEO and management board roles in very successful companies, we kept in contact as we enjoyed each other's company. And every time, I heard this phrase spoken in a business setting, I remembered him and thought about how so many people misunderstood this phrase.

Nearly 15 years later, I had the pleasure to spend another weekend with him, along with other former friends/colleagues. During one conversation, I said to him, "Remember how you told us to keep an eye on the ball? I did that throughout most of my career, and it helped me to achieve whatever I set up in my mind. But, unfortunately, I witnessed the opposite practice by many leaders.

To use another analogy, they kept their eyes only on the cake, not on the people who were baking the cake. Those leaders were only interested in getting a piece of the cake. What do you think about that?"

He looked at me with great surprise and said, "I guess there will always be very hungry people on this planet who eat more than their share – and people do need to eat. But you know that very successful businesses are only built by people who engender trust with their clients as well as their own people. If you lose sight of this point, you are in trouble. Stick with building trust. And don't forget that 'people' means clients, your colleagues, and your employees. So, my friend, continue to keep your eyes on the ball – keep your eyes on the people!"

REFERENCES

Deloitte

Empoweredbusiness.com

Forbes.com

Gallup

Gallup Business Journal

Global Employee Benefits Watch

Harvard Business Review

Hay Group

HR Factbook

Investopedia.com

McKinsley Quarterly

Mergerintegration.com

Netsurvey

RBC Global Asset Management

Risk Management Magazine

Saba

SHRM.org

Training Magazine

Virtuali

Visualcapitalist.com

Workplacetrends.com

INDEX

Topic	Chapter
Barriers to success	5
Branding	10
Corporate spending	3, 4
Disengaged employees	1, 8, 9
Emerging markets	11
Generations	11
Leadership	1, 2, 5, 8, 10
Mergers and acquisitions	6
Mis-hires	4
Shareholders	5, 7
sparkChief	14, 15, 16, 17
Talent agent	9
Technology	13, 14, 15
Transparency	7
Untapped resources	11

www.ingramcontent.com/pod-product-compliance
Lightning Source LLC
Chambersburg PA
CBHW020427220526
45464CB00002B/600